Arnhem Doctor

Arnhem Doctor

by

Stuart Mawson

Foreword by General Sir John Hackett

SPELLMOUNT
Staplehurst

British Library Cataloguing in Publication Data:
A catalogue record for this book is available
from the British Library

Copyright © Stuart Mawson 1981, 2000

ISBN 1-86227-088-0

First published by Orbis Publishing Ltd in 1981
This edition first published in the UK in 2000 by
Spellmount Limited
The Old Rectory
Staplehurst
Kent TN12 0AZ

1 3 5 7 9 8 6 4 2

Printed in Great Britain by
T. J. International Ltd
Padstow, Cornwall

Contents

And ere a man hath power to say 'behold'
The jaws of darkness do devour it up:
So quick bright things come to confusion.

A Midsummer Night's Dream
Act I, Scene II

Foreword

by General Sir John Hackett

We in Britain call it the Battle of Arnhem. This is not inappropriate, since the seizure and retention of the road bridge over the Lower Rhine at Arnhem, in September 1944, was the whole purpose of the 1st Airborne Division's operation. The Dutch, however, commonly refer to it as the Battle of Arnhem-Oosterbeek, which is perhaps more accurate. The northern end of Arnhem Bridge was in fact seized and held for four days by Frost's 2nd Parachute Battalion, one of Lathbury's in the First Parachute Brigade. In the event the defenders, short of everything they needed and now desperately weak in numbers, were overwhelmed. When the Bridge was lost, however, the battle was far from over. The rest of the division continued to defend the bridgehead in and around Oosterbeek village for four more hard-fought days, the perimeter defence being divided between two Brigade Commands, the 1st Airlanding Brigade under Pip Hicks, and the 4th Parachute Brigade, which was mine. It was in the fighting there, five miles downstream from the Bridge itself, that the division bled almost to death. Practically none among the very heavy casualties of the Oosterbeek fighting in the bridgehead ever got anywhere near the Bridge. Few even saw it.

Whatever it is called, this battle, nearly forty years on, continues to exercise a strong hold on the public imagination and books are still being written about it. Here is another, but not just another: this one is something special. It is an account of the experiences of a young parachuting Regimental Medical Officer, unavoidably separated from his battalion and drawn by circumstances into the action at a Dressing Station located in the very eye of the battle. This was at the crossing where the road from Arnhem to Utrecht comes into Oosterbeek, fiercely fought over and round and through, and changing hands more than once as one side or the other gained the advantage. The basic narrative was set down by the author in note form shortly afterwards and written up soon after the war ended, when detail was still fresh in his mind. The script has been revised and published now that the author has retired, after a full life in surgical practice, from consultancy in a famous London hospital. It is a simple, authentic and poignant document, a testament to man's humanity in the inhumanity of war and to the combination of fortitude, devotion, discipline and professional skill, that makes of the Royal Army Medical Corps something of which not only the British Army but the whole nation can be proud.

I am grateful to be allowed to write this foreword not only because I, too, was a casualty in that battle and owe my life to the RAMC, but because I was actually engaged for much of it at the very place of which the author writes and was deeply involved in what went on there. The hotel-restaurant, the Schoonoord, in which the Dressing Station was set up, was right in the middle of what became the front line of my thinly held brigade sector. Brigade head quarters, throughout the Oosterbeek fighting, was only a few hundred yards up the road, first of all in a house and then in holes in the ground around it. I saw the Schoonoord every day and was in it several times. The author speaks, for example, of trees nearby and of some anti-tank guns of ours among them, only a few paces away from the Dressing Station, when it already held three or four hundred wounded. How well I remember going down to the sergeant in charge of those two guns and telling him he would have to come back out of it, for an attack was imminent and our 17-pounders were too precious to lose – and his very firm reply! I might be the Brigadier, he said and implied that I might even be God Almighty, but he was not going to move those guns back until the CRA* of the division, his own Brigadier, ordered him to do so.

The 11th Parachute Battalion, the unit in which Mawson was the RMO and which was commanded by George Lea, one of the very best officers you could find anywhere, was detailed from my brigade, as soon as we landed in the second lift on 18th September, to go forward as a reinforcement to help Frost at the Bridge. In the unavoidable absence of the Divisional Commander from Div. HQ the battalion was cruelly misused. After being kept waiting around during critical hours, when a determined move towards the Bridge in good time might just have saved the situation, it was sent off at night, with no clearer orders than to do the best it could with other

*Commander Royal Artillery

detachments similarly sent off, under no joint command and with no coherent plan, into a built-up area, strange to everyone, where the enemy was gathering strength. In the inevitable confusion that followed, Mawson and his section got separated from the battalion and fetched up in the Dressing Station established in the Schoonoord by Lt-Colonel Marrable with the 181st Field Ambulance of the glider-borne Airlanding Brigade, where the arrival of another Medical Officer with part of his section was most welcome.

It has to be remembered that this was a young man who had never in his life before been out of his own country. His first venture abroad was to be dropped on the end of a parachute into an airborne battle. What is more, he came in on the second day of it when the euphoria of liberation had been largely succeeded by the grim business of fighting against a growing and determined opposition. He was already a qualified medical practitioner with some hospital experience. He had also already discovered something of what the well-ordered nature of service in any part of the British Army can do to strengthen self-discipline. His narrative discloses a growing awareness of himself, of his powers and limitations, and his swift development as a person under the pressures of battle. It was a battle, moreover, whose ferocity, a German officer told him, had never been surpassed in the German's own experience, even in Russia. His book explores with insight and detachment the effect upon a developing personality of the demands of an exacting professional discipline, within the structure of army requirements.

Personal relationships grow and flourish in such a situation as in a forcing-house. There are the personnel of the Medical Corps, producing order again and again in the Schoonoord Dressing Station, in their own dedicated way, out of gross and cruelly and violently renewed disorder; there are the devoted Dutch, the men and even more the women; there is the slight and sensitively drawn figure, luminously attractive, of the young Dutch nurse, supremely brave and calm; there is Stuart Mawson's own emergence from a young man, professionally well-equipped, into a man not only of deep humanity but of substance and of consequence.

There are lessons in this book for everyone. Simply written, it is likely, in my opinion, to become one of the more important small memoirs of the Second World War.

Professional competence, humanity, fortitude and unbounded hope make up a good prescription for the future health of mankind. In this book, *Arnhem Doctor,* they are all abundantly dispensed.

Author's Note

This book is not intended to be an accurate, detailed history of the battle – for that can be found elsewhere – but an account, recalled as honestly as possible, of the personal experience of someone who was a very minor link in the chain of doctors privileged to give their services on that occasion. It has been compiled from notes and a narrative put together soon after, in 1945, and from old newspaper cuttings, photographs and, of course, from memory. I have tried to preserve the 'feel' of those momentous days and to avoid distorting my original impressions by adding corrections of hindsight. If the events seem confused it can be accepted as a reflection of my own state of mind at the time. If there are inaccuracies in the light of the now known facts, it is because the only facts I was aware of then were those affecting myself. I have no special qualifications for writing on the subject other than having taken part, and I fear lest I may not have given every man mentioned his due. But if it can be seen how the Royal Army Medical Corps coped tirelessly with appalling difficulties and did its utmost for the wounded, I shall be content to stand corrected on any errors or shortcomings which other participants may detect in this account.

Prologue

2 April 1979. It is a Monday morning, but something is different. I
sit up in bed. My wife is still asleep. Yet it is a quarter to seven and I
should be getting up, starting the day's proceedings preparatory to
leaving for the hospital. I have to arrive there by half past eight, in
order to deal with paper work, habitually falling to my lot every
morning as chairman of various committees, before beginning on
my operating list. No alarm call; that was it. The clock had not been
set and the bell had not rung. 'A lucky thing I woke,' I tell myself,
'knowing my tendency to oversleep after the week-end.' Then I hear
a commotion of birds outside the window. I rise and draw the
curtains. I am in the country, not in London. The implication dawns
and my memory clears. Yesterday I said goodbye to the hospital. All
the pages of my life as a consultant surgeon at King's College
Hospital, London, have been turned, and I am beginning a new
chapter. I do not have to get up and go anywhere. I am retired. I go
back to bed.

Lying there, musing and looking back over my career I felt I had
some grounds for satisfaction at having stayed the course thus far.
But in the formation of my career there was one episode I would
wish to recall and record, which began on another Monday morning
thirty-five years ago, when I awoke with a similar awareness that
something was different.

Monday 18 September 1944

I was a Captain in the Royal Army Medical Corps, the Regimental Medical Officer to the 11th Parachute Battalion of the 4th Brigade, the 1st Airbourne Division, asleep in my quarters in England when the bugle sounded reveille. I shared the quarters in England, the Inspection Room Block, a custom-built wooden building, with my Medical Sergeant, Sergeant Dwyer, and my batman, Private Adams. Reveille was normally the signal for Adams to get up and prepare tea, Dwyer to light a first cigarette and myself to turn over and go to sleep again. My rank gave me the privilege of shaving and dressing last while the other two were getting things ready for the morning Sick Parade.

But this morning I did not go to sleep again. I heard the bugle dimly as usual and opened one eye to glance at the luminous dial of my watch. Five-thirty! I looked again. Why so early? I turned over to reach for the light switch and, propping myself on my elbow, caught sight of a stack of unfamiliar objects by the bed. There was already a pale light filtering through the window, and after blinking at the objects for a few seconds I subsided slowly back onto the pillow. Of course! The big kit-bag, haversack braces and pouches, water bottle and pistol lying on the floor, the clean underwear and shirt on the chair, I had put them out the night before. I wanted to recoil back into myself and to postpone the harsh significance of those things, for they made an impact altogether too abrupt and disturbing to be reckoned with just yet. I turned my head towards the window and gazed at the grey mist-veiled sky. There were about five hours left before there was any need to worry. Five hours in which everything would be quite normal, plenty of time to compose oneself, plenty of time to get used to things. I could begin by lying in bed until Adams brought the tea, and accustom myself to the implications of the day.

I had qualified as a doctor eighteen months previously at the age of twenty-four, then, after six months as a very junior doctor in a big London Teaching Hospital, had been called up to the army. A fortnight after joining the army I had volunteered for the special unit to which I now belonged. If asked what made me do it, I could not have given a precise reply. The answer I gave the recruiting officer had been that other chaps from the hospital had been in it from the start and it seemed a good thing to keep the tradition going. But that was only a small part of the truth.

I rolled my head back to look at the equipment by the bed. Strange that such a pile of inanimate objects could betoken so much; the thought that had gone into their selection, the hands that had made them, their assembling from various stores, and at last their placing in readiness for wearing today. Very soon I would have to put them on and follow the remorseless unfolding of events that history had prepared. It was all very well trying not to think of what lay ahead but detachment does not come easily unless the mind is very practised, and I was glad when at length I heard Adams coming with the tea. He banged on the door, came in and set a mug down noisily on the floor by the bed, gripped my shoulder in a proprietary manner and, shaking me, roughly announced:

'Char's up, sir. Char's up.'

I yawned, ran my hands through my hair and then sat up, regarding him with the growing good humour that his morning appearance regularly promoted. He was a cockney born and bred, short, dark and sturdy, with a somewhat mournful expression emphasized by a moustache of which, I had been told, he was inordinately proud. He was a discreet but expert scrounger and, although only in his very early twenties, seemed very old and knowing for his age. He never showed any resentment at being what the army would regard as my servant and was always most solicitous for my welfare, looking after my needs and equipment with commendable thoroughness. As a medical clerk he was a dependable keeper of records, returns in triplicate, treatment cards and inoculation registers. He sat with me in the sick parades and never missed a trick. From the medical knowledge thus gained he founded a clandestine medical practice of his own. Men who did not care to go sick officially would seek him out privately and ask his advice. He was also regarded by them as a reliable channel of information for some of the unpublished aspects of Battalion affairs.

'Thank you, Adams. How's the exercise going?'

9

'All OK, sir. Sergeant's shaving. There are a lot of chaps already on the parade ground. Weather's good and it really does look as though we shall be going this time – at last.'

He shifted his eyes to the floor, then looked up diffidently and asked, 'What do you think it will be like, sir?'

I wanted to reply, 'Wish I knew,' but it would not do to share my private thoughts with Adams. Officers were supposed to put on a front of infallibility. Leadership depended upon certainty of action at every point. I knew I was Adams's leader not only because of my rank but for the very simple reason that by no stretch of the imagination could I ever conceive of Adams leading me. So I replied, 'Well you heard the report on yesterday's lift, it will obviously be a piece of cake.'

'You don't think, sir, there's a chance the 1st Brigade will have done it all by now and we'll be stood down yet again?' Adams looked genuinely anxious. The possibility had been in everyone's mind at the briefing. There had been so many actions called off at the last minute, and the whole Battalion including myself were raring to go.

'We'll just have to take everything as it comes,' I said, trying to sound confident. 'From what you tell me, things are going ahead, so let's get ready. Tell Sergeant Dwyer I'll be along shortly.'

I drank the tea, threw back the bedclothes and slithered out of bed. I had myself advised that everyone should put on clean underwear. It wasn't merely that it might have to be worn for several days on end, but that much of the contamination of wounds resulted from clothing carried in with the missile. I could not suppress a slight shudder as I donned my own white vest. It reminded me of the preparations that are made for an operation, when the skin, shaved and purified with surgical spirit, may be covered with a sterile towel until the last moment when it is exposed to the surgeon's knife. I felt better as soon as I had my trousers on and my vulnerable parts were no longer exposed. Once into the steel-shod boots and webbing gaiters I clumped firmly about the room collecting the necessary materials for washing and shaving. In the Medical Inspection room Sergeant Dwyer was wiping the last remnants of soap from behind his ears.

'Morning, Sergeant,' I greeted him.

'Morning, sir.'

'Have you heard of any changes in the overnight arrangements?'

'No, sir. I've just phoned Orderly Room and there's been nothing new in from Brigade.'

'OK. Then we've still got a couple of hours to have breakfast and get loaded up. Better have a good breakfast' – at this Dwyer made a grimace of disgust – 'no matter how you feel after last night's party. There's no knowing when we shall get our next proper meal.'

We would each be carrying two of the small cartons containing twenty-four hours' rations – concentrated oatmeal, meat cubes, boiled sweets, plain chocolate, cigarettes, benzedrine tablets, and a preconstituted powder of tea-leaves, milk powder and sugar ready-mixed for the addition of hot water. It would satisfy hunger, support life and provide energy for two days. Sergeant Dwyer was more optimistic. He always was. Again, like Adams, he was short, sturdy and moustached, but unlike in being fair-haired and jaunty, with an aggressive deportment and a smile that taunted and deceived; deceived because its readiness might tempt the taking of liberties, which would have been unwise. Dwyer was tough physically and mentally. He had had battle experience of which I knew I was going to be thankful.

'Don't you worry, sir,' he said. 'There'll be bags of food in the houses and smiling girls all the way offering us fruit and wine.'

'Could be,' I thought, 'could very well be.'

I took elaborate care over my shaving. Anything that emphasized the normal helped to dispel the air of unreality that seemed to hang over the morning. I felt strangely ill at ease, as though wearing a suit that was not my own and did not fit anywhere. For one thing it was difficult to rid oneself of a constant awareness of the passing of time. As if the very desire to think as little as possible of the future led to a perverse persistence of it in the mind. While one part of me was impatient to have done with waiting and get on with it, the other lingered over every detail of the commonplace, reluctant to meet the unknown and unfamiliar.

After a leisurely breakfast of eggs and bacon in the Officers' Mess to which I did full justice, never having been put entirely off my food at any crisis of my life, I returned once more to the Medical Block to take the Sick Parade. I did not anticipate a large attendance, if indeed any at all. There were always one or two chronic malingerers, even in the crack units, who would from time to time evade their duties by simulating illness. They knew all the tricks and usually complained of vague symptoms, such as backache, which were difficult to disprove, but it was practically unknown for anyone to report sick on the morning of action, and so it turned out. No one came to see me officially, although two or three men consulted Adams privately about a certain looseness of the bowels which they feared might prove an embarrassment later on. After that, I called him into my bedroom to help me on with my equipment. I already had the camouflage smock on and was struggling into the webbing. One's back had to be left clear for the parachute, so the main haversack was carried on the chest, high up under the chin. Below this on either side were ammunition pouches, filled with dressings and bandages. On one hip hung a second haversack and on the other a revolver and map case. By the time the tin crash-helmet had been clamped on the head one felt fully burdened enough without the great kit-bag which still, later on, had to be strapped to the right leg for the jump. In this kit-bag was a large alpine rucksack, full of medical supplies, which would be carried on the back instead of the parachute, once the latter was discarded.

'Now,' I said to Adams, 'let me help you on with your stuff and we'll go and see how Sergeant is getting on.'

When the three of us were ready, we went out of the Medical Inspection Room for the last time and, staggering under our loads, started walking across to the waiting motor transports which were drawn up in ranks on the further side of the parade ground, onto which the whole Battalion was converging from the barrack huts, each man festooned with weapons and equipment. We were met by the Major commanding Headquarter Company.

The Battalion had four companies, A, B, C and HQ, the latter incorporating the administrative nerve centre to which I, as the Battalion Medical Officer, was attached. There were sixteen Royal Army Medical Corps other ranks, a corporal to each company with a quota of stretcher bearers, whose task in battle was to collect the wounded and bring them to me wherever I had established my Regimental Aid Post with Dwyer, Adams and the rest of my own medical section. These arrangements were common to each of the six parachute and three glider-borne battalions in the 1st Airborne Division. Backing us up at brigade level (three battalions to each brigade) were the Field Ambulances intended to operate as independent Dressing Stations back from the 'front', equipped with surgical teams and airborne jeep ambulances. They also provided intermediate links with the Regimental Aid Posts through the setting up and staffing of Casualty Clearing Posts if the distance between 'front' and 'rear' so demanded. My job was, in effect, to administer first aid and hold the casualties until they could be moved back to the Dressing Station via the Casualty Clearing Post, or directly to the former as circumstances permitted.

Major Dan Webber, commanding HQ Company, was a very competent, battle-experienced officer newly acquired by the battalion, with whom I had already established a good working relation. Never given to verbosity he greeted me briefly. 'Hallo, Doc. Your boys all ready?'

'All OK, Dan. How's everything going?'

'Fine. We're due to move off in about ten minutes so will you get loaded up.'

I helped Dwyer and Adams to climb in over the tail-board of the lorry we were to travel in and then, with some difficulty, humped myself up into the front seat beside the driver. I had hardly settled in when Pat Crawford, the Intelligence Officer, came by and offered me a newspaper. Pat and I had been at the same public school together. He had a narrow, rather foxy face and a nose for information that went with it. He was not tall but very wiry, as were so many paratroopers, and a great leg-puller.

'Read all about yesterday, Doc. It's all in here, buck you up a treat.'

We had a brief conversation and then I settled back in the lorry and looked at the paper. It had the airborne landings of the two American Divisions and the 1st British Brigade spread all over the front page. Correspondents who had gone in with them had sent up-to-date versions of the actions. 'It was the greatest aerial effort of all time, and the airborne landing was much larger than the D-Day operation. Thousands of Allied aircraft were over Holland yesterday, and our losses were negligible. The landings were accomplished under ideal weather and, thanks to tremendous day and night bombing before the gigantic operation, there was only meagre anti-aircraft opposition and no interference at all from the Luftwaffe.' Reference was made to the awe-inspiring sight of the slow, majestic, relentless advance of endless squadrons of troop-carrying C 47s, Dakotas, carrying paratroopers and towing gliders, the message of invincibility coming through strong and clear. I read on, 'Not a single Dakota lost.' 'Only other Allied aircraft in the sky were Allied fighters forming an armoured aerial tunnel for the transports.' 'All first objectives taken.' 'Surprise of the enemy complete.'

It all seemed too good to be true, but the dope began to work, tuning my mind to reception of the belief that why, after all, should not today be as yesterday. Why not? I thought of the times we had been briefed and had not gone, sixteen in all, just because the enemy resistance to the liberation army collapsed before we were required. It was quite possible the 1st Brigade had got to the Bridge by now, and all we would have to do would be to march in and sit round it until tomorrow as planned. There might not even be a single casualty if what the paper said was true.

Then the driver climbed in beside me.

'We're off now,' he announced.

I gave the thumbs up sign to the Adjutant, Captain Peter Milo, who had signed me a query as to whether we were ready, and after a short pause the convoy began to move off. At the entrance to the camp the rear party stood stiffly to attention and saluted as the convoy passed. We dipped downhill into Melton Mowbray, which was just rubbing the sleep from its eyes, and then struck out across mist-pocketed country towards the airfield. I knew the road well, having on several occasions driven out to this particular airfield to take part in exercises and practice drops. I watched the familiar landmarks appear and go by without really consciously noting their passage, saying nothing to the driver and sitting still, except occasionally to ease my position away from some hard piece of equipment. One was the helpless straw in the wind, the stick in the current. What else was there to do except just sit and be carried along?

My mind went idling into the past, like the countryside, and a train of thought, which began with the realization that none of my relations, or friends outside the Battalion, knew exactly where I was or what I was doing at that moment, took me thumbing back through the pages of memory to my days as a student at St Thomas's Hospital where the seed was sown that, together with deeper and less well understood motives, resulted in my involvement in the Parachute Regiment. Across the road from the hospital main entrance was a public house, the Two Sawyers, where we students were wont to quench our thirst after the day's activities. One evening we were joined by Charles Granville Rob who had been a Resident Surgical Officer at the Hospital and who had become one of the first of the surgeons in the Royal Army Medical Corps to see action with the 1st Airborne Division. He had won the MC and been wounded in North Africa and was now home on leave. He put it to us, gathered in the pub, that it would be a good thing if the

Airborne Forces were able to call on Thomas's chaps to staff their medical units, and asked how would we feel about volunteering after we were qualified. I remembered we all seemed to have agreed that it would be a great idea and then had forgotten the incident, until the pay-off came after I had been called up to the army and was at the RAMC Training Depot at Crookham. There my class received a visit from Brigadier Eagger, Deputy Director of Medical Services of the 1st British Airborne Corps, who appeared to have my number and who singled me out as having already shown interest. He had played skilfully on my liking for sailing and rugby football and suggested how apt such activities were in relation to parachuting, and without giving the matter really serious consideration I had gone in. It had all seemed a bit of a lark, a newly qualified junior doctor in those days being not far removed developmentally from an overgrown schoolboy. But once absorbed into the paratroops one became shaped and moulded into something rather different. The larks were still there, especially on mess nights, but the responsibilities changed.

On first putting on the uniform of a soldier, with only the RAMC shoulder flashes and cap badge to remind me of my true profession, and learning at the Depot of the unavoidable restraints placed on a soldier/doctor's freedom to act independently as a doctor, I felt somewhat schizophrenic: split between the hospital teaching, that patients' needs take priority over everything, and the military reality, that ideals of treatment, convalescence and rehabilitation must often be restricted in order to return a man back into the line as soon as possible. I chafed for a time under this curtailment of what I had been trained to understand as a doctor's freedom to prescribe. But the logic of the circumstances gradually seeped through. The freedoms of civvy street were among the things we were fighting for. Soldiers were needed to achieve victory. Soldiers had to be treated within the demanding framework of war-time soldiering by those who understood war-time soldiering. With this understanding I began to feel more and more at ease in my uniform.

I came to learn the interdependence of men upon each other and the vital importance of team work, to understand the necessity for my particular role and to gain the confidence that the habit of discipline, inculcated by the army, would enable me to carry it out. I had experienced great fear during parachute training but the system had seen me through. My ego gradually underwent submersion in the greater unity of the Corps and with it came a satisfaction and happiness never experienced before. The essence of the life was its simplicity. Personal problems reduced themselves to a minimum. The relationship between myself and others in the unit was beautifully simple. All ranks knew their places, and in the Officers' Mess there was a camaraderie maintained by custom, which avoided discussion of deep or controversial matters, and approved cheerfulness and the minimization of hardship and danger.

The previous night in the mess had been especially hilarious, even though it was the night before the day when we knew in sober reality that we might all be exposed to an ordeal of probable pain and possible death, certainly of fear – 'it'. Friendships were heightened by the underlying threat to their continuity. There was instinctive demonstration of mutual regard, arms were thrown round shoulders, backs slapped, glasses clinked, smiles readily given and jokes loudly applauded. There was also a subtle parade of manhood, an unconscious swagger in the manner of drinking. Everyone had spent the evening on their feet, welcoming each new entrant to the mess with noisy demonstrations and escortings to the bar. There was a press representative told off to accompany us who, being a stranger, was especially fêted. We made him welcome and tried to make him feel as one of us, sensing that the experience for him on the morrow would be tougher than for ourselves, who had prepared for and expected nothing else for weeks.

The morning was windless and the mist still lay very thick in places. It seemed likely in view of this that the take-off would be postponed and I fretted at the prospect of any delay, wanting to come to grips with the thing now as soon as possible. In the back of the vehicle, no doubt, Dwyer and Adams would be keeping up their spirits with reminiscences and anecdotes, possibly of other airborne actions of which they had experience, more probably of amorous escapades in various places. My imagination became busy with trying to picture again what being in action would be like, the wounds I would have to deal with and in what circumstances I would be working, but I could not see much beyond the training exercises I had taken part in, and had an uncomfortable feeling they were in no way to be compared with the real thing.

The convoy of forty or more transports, carrying the Battalion of over nine hundred men, wound up a short but steep hill on the Grantham-to-Lincoln road, and then took a sharp turn to the right. As the transports rose out of the vale the mist thinned, and in a very short time those in the leading vehicles could discern the boundaries of the airfield, and an airsock flapping idly on its mast. The convoy drove onto the perimeter, which was packed with C 47s, and then scattered; each individual transport made for one of the Dakotas and disgorged its load of men beside it. I lowered myself from the vehicle with the encumbered deliberation of a diver going into the sea, and once on the ground stamped about restoring circulation, while watching the men climb over the tailboard and drop with a creak and clank onto the tarmac. I singled out Dwyer.

'OK. Form the stick* up here, Sergeant,' I told him. 'Major Webber will shortly want to inspect equipment.'

They sorted themselves out into two lines alongside the Dakota, men of the Headquarter Company who would form part of the vital administrative nucleus of the 11th Battalion's action. The Commanding Officer, Lt-Col. George Lea, now at a brigade briefing, would go in this aeroplane with the Intelligence Officer and the Signals Sergeant. The rest of the stick, apart from Dwyer, Adams and myself, consisted of a group of men under an NCO whose concern was the defence of the Command Post wherever it happened to be set up. In another Dakota the Second-in-Command, Major Richard Lonsdale, would fly with a shadow organization, ready to take over in the event of any disaster overtaking the CO's plane. Major Webber, commanding Headquarter Company, now appeared in a jeep, in which he had been driving round the perimeter checking over the plane-loads of men and material.

'Bring them to attention, Sergeant,' I said.

'Number one stick. Stick 'shun,' roared Dwyer, pushing out his chest as far as the Red-Cross haversack reposing on it would allow; although a small man, compact and yeasty, he enjoyed the men's respect and never had any trouble in exerting his authority. 'What a good man to have with me,' I thought; 'he seems to be taking all this in his stride.'

Webber stepped out of the jeep and took the salute.

'Everything OK, Doc?'

'Yes. All OK. How long before take-off?'

'About another half-hour, I think, but the men can fall out when I've inspected them. George Lea's still at Brigade; when he joins you, you'll know we're off. Keep an eye on my Dakota over there' – he indicated one which lay four bays down the perimeter – 'and

---

*A number of paratroops carried in one plane.

when you see my stick emplaning, get yours on board.'

He then walked up and down the two ranks of men, briefly examining weapons, parachute harness, ammunition pouches and rations. That part was only a formality as the NCOs would have checked all that back on the parade ground. The main point was to demonstrate yet again the concern of an officer for the men under his command, a concern that was at the core of officer training and a linchpin of the British system. As he leaped into his jeep and drove away Dwyer fell the men out, and they sat or stood in small groups round the Dakota, resigned to the business of waiting.

To be able to wait without impatience is a prime necessity in war. At any time of the day there are far more men waiting to fight than actually fighting, more ingenuity being expended in the invention of ways and means to occupy the lulls than in conducting the battles. Adams went into a huddle with the CO's batman, while I strolled over to the American crew of the Dakota, who were standing by the starboard engine.

'Did you go in yesterday?' I asked.

'Sure,' one of them replied, 'we went in.'

'Did you meet much opposition?'

'Not what we'd call opposition. No fighters. Just a bit of flak. It was a piece of cake.'

'Think it'll be like that today?' I was keen to check up on the newspaper reports at first hand. He paused.

'Yeah, I guess so. Only the krauts will be expecting us and there may be more stuff coming up from the ground.' He turned to the other members of the crew who nodded in agreement.

As they showed no outward concern at the prospect of an increase in anti-aircraft fire I found the conversation reassuring. 'Just the day then for parachuting,' I quipped. 'Ever tried a drop?'

'Me? Not on your life, brother. I like to have wings on when I'm in the air.'

'Can't say I blame you. Well won't be long now.'

I suddenly remembered about the air-sickness tablets and beckoned to Adams. 'Adams, the hyoscine, have you dished it out yet?'

'Only to CO's batman, sir. The others don't seem to think they'll need any.'

I was thankful that air sickness was something I never suffered from. The flight was scheduled to last two and a half hours so that there would indeed be time for the susceptible to feel the effects.

There would also be plenty of time for all to develop those familiar but uncomfortable symptoms of increasing apprehension, inseparable from the approach of danger. To some, fear would come only at the last moment. Others, unable to prevent their thoughts ranging ahead, would suffer earlier; for the imagination is frequently more fear-provoking than the event. On the other hand for the latter the event, when it did arrive, often came as an anti-climax with a lessening of tension and a sense of relief. I hopefully placed myself in the last category as I was already feeling a build-up of anxiety. But not as much as I had expected. Not only had the demands of this special occasion acted as a booster, so that, especially in the company of others, I felt buoyed up, even at times exhilarated, but there was also the repeated conditioning, at first by the briefing, then by the radio and press and now from my conversation with the crew, that enabled one to believe, really believe, in the majestic invincibility of the operation. To me, and no doubt to nine tenths, at least, of all those waiting for the flight to begin, the outcome was so far from being in doubt that we foresaw only a rather glorified exercise, with the marked probability that, when we had marched the five miles from the dropping zone to Arnhem, we would have the chagrin of finding Monty and the liberation army already there with nothing left to be done at all. It was to be a field day with a spice of adventure added. The fighting men had unlimited confidence in themselves, and found it perfectly natural that their catchname, the 'Red Devils', should strike awe and respect into their opponents.

After what seemed like an endless period of tedious waiting and aimless talk, Sergeant Dwyer said, 'I see the Company Commander's beginning to emplane. Shall I fall the stick in, sir?'

I looked over to confirm.

'Thank you. Right away.'

'Come along then, number one stick. Let's have you.' Dwyer was employing his best parade ground voice again. 'Fall in in double ranks, look slippy.'

The men started fastening their equipment, which they had eased off for comfort, and lugging their kit-bags formed up on the port side of the Dakota with their backs to the fuselage and door.

'Properly at ease everywhere,' Dwyer continued the drill. 'Stick, stick 'shun.'

He went round each of the two ranks, inspecting equipment, especially parachute fastenings, and then turned and saluted. 'Stick present and correct, sir.'

'Right. Emplane, Sergeant.'

Dwyer gave them a left turn into line and the men began to enter through the wide door, now on their left, that opened into the fuselage just forward of the tailplane. Once inside, the stick divided itself into two rows, passing forward between the metal seats, lining each side of the compartment. They were numbered off into odds and evens, one group on each side. The first man to go in was number twenty, seated nearest to the pilot's compartment, opposite was number nineteen and so on. Colonel Lea would occupy the number one seat, next to the door, myself beside him in number three seat, and Pat Crawford the Intelligence officer on my left side in number five. Opposite sat our respective batmen, now already in position. I waited on the tarmac with Dwyer, gazing in the direction from which the Colonel was expected to appear with Crawford, who had also been attending final Brigade briefing. The air was full of the clatter and roar of starting and revving engines, including our own, and ordinary conversation was impossible. Some Dakotas were already beginning to move, preparatory to taking up their positions on the runway, and soon we caught sight of a jeep speeding away from the administration block in our direction. Shortly it was near enough to distinguish the figure of the CO, waving to each aircraft as he passed and shouting something that I guessed was 'Good luck, Battalion'.

The jeep fretted to a standstill and, as the CO swung his tall frame onto the tarmac, I saluted and said, 'Stick emplaned. All present and correct, sir.' Then I added as an afterthought, 'Very glad to see you.'

'Glad to be here, Doc,' he replied briskly. 'Has my man got all my stuff on board? Here,' and, without waiting for an answer, he handed a map to Crawford who had climbed out of the jeep after him, 'tell him to put this on top of the others in my case. Now then, all ready? Let's go.'

He stepped up into the Dakota, followed by the rest of us, and passed up between the rows of men, putting in a word here and there as he made his way forward to the pilot and crew's compartment. I addressed myself to the Intelligence officer, 'Anything new, Pat?'

'Nothing much. The 1st Brigade are having quite a fight for it on the Bridge, but from our point of view that's a help as it means they will be keeping what enemy troops there are there too busy to bother us. The gen is Jerry must be expecting us but won't be able to muster much opposition.'

At the same time as Colonel Lea re-emerged from the pilot's compartment the plane started to vibrate intensely, as the thrust of the engines was increased for taxying. We started to move, swinging this way and that, accelerating one minute and stopping jerkily the next as we jockeyed into position for the runway. Some planes were already airborne, others were queueing nose to tail to take their run. There were often as many as three on the runway at the same time in the process of taking off.

In each Dakota was a despatcher, a member of the American crew, whose business it was at this stage to see that the trim of the aircraft was properly maintained by the even distribution of its cargo, human and material, and to act as a link between the pilot and commanding officer. Later he would have the duty of giving the order to leave the plane at the time of the drop, and of seeing that the stick went out in an orderly fashion. During practice take-offs the stick would press up towards the nose end of the plane to assist the lifting of the tail, but now, owing to the mass of battle equipment with which each man was festooned, there was no room to do more than sit wedged in the travelling position, which seemed to upset the despatcher who, gesticulating, shouted, 'Move up, fellas, if you can. We're doo for take-off right now.'

The best we could do was to lean a little sideways and, as the aircraft gathered speed, were hard put to it to do even that. The engines were thundering and the wings could be seen through the windows shuddering with the effort. The rapid acceleration as we sped down the runway had the unwanted effect of pressing everybody towards the tail. I held my breath. Surely we should be airborne by now. I wondered if the plane were not too heavily loaded, recalling other flights when we seemed to be in the air almost at once, and, as the seconds dragged by and the rumbling contact between wheels and ground resonated through my body, the picture flashed onto the screen of my mind of a tangled mass of wreckage with myself somewhere in the middle of it. Then I felt her come free and, looking down through the window, saw fields, hedges and trees streaming away beneath us. There were a few more anxious moments as we made height, climbing in wide banking circles – for a plane is like a ship, the further it is away from land in its own element the safer it is – and then we were well up, still circling around, waiting for all the other Dakotas to become airborne and complete the Battalion formation of which we would be leader.

Colonel Lea, as the first to jump, sat nearest the open door on his right, and I could see past him and through it, as it framed quite a large view of the sky, which was divided into two by the tailplane beneath which we all must pass as we jumped out. Astern of us, as far as I could see, were echelons of Dakotas flying in regular terraces one above the other, and by the time the formation was established it was well nigh impossible to look astern through the door without seeing them. As we roared purposefully towards the east coast, I experienced a genuine surge of spirit. The trumpeter had sounded the charge, we had dug in our spurs, there was no turning back, now or ever.

When we were properly settled on our course the CO addressed his batman. 'Did you remember to tell the Quartermaster to post that letter for me before we left this morning?'

'Oh yes, sir. Proper cut up the Quartermaster was at having to stay behind. Said what did he join the Airborne for, if they were going to send him over by sea when all the fun was over.'

'Do you think this is fun?' asked the Colonel, smiling. 'I don't know about you Doc, but I think he looks a bit green. Did you take the Doc's pill?'

'Yes, sir. I'll be all right. It's me stomach. It's a bit empty.'

The Colonel's smile broadened. There was a special relation between an officer and his batman. Moreover, they were about the same age, both in their very early thirties. Old in comparison with the average age of the stick but, of course, young in terms of a normal lifetime.

I turned to help the CO as he started to don his equipment. It was his usual practice to spend the early part of a flight in doing so as, unlike his men, he needed to remain unencumbered to the moment of emplaning so that he could attend to the last-minute conferences and inspections that fell to his lot on an airfield. I was glad of something to do. Boredom is one of the chief enemies. I busied myself with fastenings, until finally I held the parachute strappings and he leant back into the harness and shrugged it up onto his shoulders as high as it would comfortably go. This being done, he sat down, crossed his legs, pulled out a cigarette case and handed it round to those within his immediate reach. I flicked my lighter and was glad to see the flame held steady. Lea then fell to a study of his maps and, as Crawford was engaged in conversation with his left-hand neighbour, I extracted my morning newspaper from the haversack on my thigh, where I had slipped it as the convoy set off from the camp, and began to read again.

How hard habit dies! Thousands of Englishmen everyday on their way to work read a morning newspaper. There seemed nothing incongruous to me at that moment in reading a paper with glaring headlines about something I was taking part in. We seemed to have a knack of reducing the circumstances of war into terms of everyday life, which helps us through and perhaps explains our ability to stick things out. We tame the abnormal moment by treating it as a commonplace.

I became engrossed in an article, which purported to explain how the margarine ration could be made to go further by pounding it up with the cream off the top of the milk, when Colonel Lea remarked that we were now passing over the English coast at Aldeburgh, and we would celebrate the fact with a cup of tea. We carried a store of thermos flasks and sandwiches, but the tea wasn't tea as it is understood in Mayfair or Darjeeling. It was a thick, dark brew – enough, it has been said, to make a cat speak – reinforced with condensed milk and much sugar, and its flavour was as strong as its appearance. But what it did for the army, only the army knows. It could pour morale and backbone into exhausted men, and compel a cheerful comment from the lips of the most dispirited. Of course there was a good medical explanation for this. Something hot in the stomach was a stimulus to the vegetative nervous system. The fluid replaced that lost through the sweat of fear or exertion, the sugar replenished the level in the blood and supplied energy, while the mere fact of doing something familiar and pleasant in the company of others was as reassuring as the light of a fire in the jungle that keeps the wild animals away. But a medical explanation is hardly needed for something that patently works. Adams and I shared our tea from the same mug. It was part of his job to produce sustenance for his officer at these times, whoever he might happen to be. He, therefore, dutifully handed the mug to me and waited patiently until I had finished and handed it back to him.

Having finished my sandwiches, I lit another cigarette and looked out of the window at the sea below. It was ridged like the hair of an Assyrian in a bas-relief, with a glint here and there as the sun was reflected off it. The small vessels, which could be seen raising a wake below, were, I supposed, the RAF Rescue Launches, mentioned as being in support at the Battalion briefing. I looked round the traverse of sky afforded by the window and then out of the door. There were no signs of any Allied fighters, no sign of the 'armoured aerial tunnel' that had been a reported feature of yesterday's fly-in. I voiced my surprise to Crawford, who said he imagined the fighters would be busy looking after any potential opposition between ourselves and the dropping zone, clearing the way as it were. Imagine! That was the crux of it. I had nothing to go on except imagination. Many of the others had been into action before and knew something of what to expect. But I had no experience of the reality of battle. My mind was a jumble of Field Days with the Officers Training Corps at school, of the bombing of London when I was a fire-watcher on the roof of the hospital, and of various exercises I had taken part in with the Battalion, when the discomforts had often been acute but the dangers nil. The idea of getting wounded or killed would not really take root as something that might happen to me, and I found myself unable to anticipate anything clearly beyond the actual descent which, in itself, because I had done it so often before, did not now give rise to much preliminary anxiety. We had flown over half way there without incident and the truth was I was not unduly apprehensive because no one at any time had suggested there was anything to be apprehensive about.

For a while I fell into a brown study, half waking, half sleeping, the drone of the engines having a soporific effect so that I became unconscious of the passage of time, but yet not entirely separated from the events around me. I was aware of voices and the smell of strong pipe tobacco. I blinked with lazy speculation at the faces opposite. Even in relaxed moments a doctor is apt to practise his profession and look for signs of disease or disturbance. If there were any disturbed in this aeroplane they certainly did not show it. Some were chewing gum, some apparently sleeping, some smoking and others reading newspapers. A few were looking out of the windows and one or two were talking. It was early afternoon and they looked just like men anywhere in England who might be taking it easy after the lunch break prior to resuming the day's work. Yet there was a quality that suggested their ease was studied, like actors waiting in the wings for their cue.

Even as my thoughts began to congeal and my head to nod I received a sharp dig in the ribs from Crawford and, in an instant, was fully awake and was goggling through the windows, as I heard him say, 'There they are, Doc.'

'Who? What?'

'The fighters.'

'Where?'

'Down there.'

Down! I had instinctively looked towards the sky, but looking seaward I saw a striped fuselage slide sideways below us and then oscillate, like a ship tacking, in the opposite direction. I turned to Colonel Lea who was looking out of the door. 'Can you see them, sir?'

'Yes, and I can see something else that looks to me very much like the Dutch coast. What do you think, Pat?'

Crawford looked intently for a moment. 'No doubt about it, sir, that's the Dutch coast all right.'

'Right then. Pass up the word. Prepare for action.'

The last was given with a rising inflection in the voice that unmistakably turned the conversation into a command. All the men began to stir, then to clip the static lines from their parachutes to a 'strop'.

Strops were pieces of webbing several feet long attached to a strong wire running the length of the roof of the cabin, so that when a man moved down towards the door the strop followed him. As he dropped, the static line and strop tautened and pulled the parachute out of the bag on his back. When he had dropped far enough and the parachute was completely extended, a final piece of string, with a carefully calculated breaking strain, snapped, and he fell free of the parachute bag, static line and strop which remained attached to the plane. It was patently a vital matter for the linkage between static line and strop to be faultless, and it was something that each man tested and re-tested with the greatest of care for his life literally depended on it. The next thing was to examine the parachute of the man in front and make sure that the run of his static line, for the time being folded in the neck of the parachute pack, was not likely to become fouled by equipment. Finally the kit-bags, which for comfort had been detached from our right legs, were strapped on again, and the twenty-foot line from which it would be suspended made fast to our belts. It felt like a ton weight, but having swung it out through the door, as though kicking a football, there was no choice but to follow. Once in a controlled descent it was unstrapped from the leg and lowered to the end of its line, so that it hit the ground first and helped to break the force of landing. All that then remained was to haul in the line, take out the contents whatever they happened to be – in my case the alpine rucksack – and the man was ready for action.

I was glad to feel I was in a position to jump out of the plane. Nobody could consider a Dakota the ideal aircraft in which to fly low over enemy-held territory, since it was singularly vulnerable to every form of attack, but the ability to escape from it at short notice now gave me a feeling of security to offset this disadvantage. I did not analyse my feelings sufficiently to realize that such an attitude compared unfavourably with the determination of the pilots and crews, who were mentally committed to fly their planes to the target and back, or go down with them. But then I was not yet truly mentally committed to the possible necessity of myself being required as a sacrifice in the cause of the war.

Preparations completed, we all tried to relax in our seats, but with our eyes glued to a window. At first Holland seemed to consist of nothing but floods; acres of land were inundated, with here and there a farmstead lying isolated amid a small island of flotsam. There was no sign of life anywhere to be seen, no livestock, no people, no enemy. Every now and then an Allied fighter would slip in and out of view, but for some ten minutes the scene remained quite desolate until my attention was drawn to a field where one of our gliders lay forlornly like a child's broken toy in an empty playground. There was nobody to be seen in the vicinity and I wondered what had happened to its occupants, as we were still some way from the target. I looked at my watch. It was a quarter to two in the afternoon and a quarter of an hour away from the estimated time of the drop.

That was the last I knew of time, except as something that passed excruciatingly slowly and seemed interminable. Momentarily I had the comfortable illusion of being in a railway carriage, for there came a tap-tapping noise like the man going the length of the train and sounding the wheels, distant at first but steadily approaching until he suddenly seemed to take leave of his senses and start slamming about with his hammer at everything in sight, and the comfort abruptly departed. Crawford answered my raised eyebrows. 'Only tracer,' he said disdainfully as a stream of incandescent bullets curved past my window into the sky.

The thought of what might happen if they came through the seat touched off an urgent desire to stand up. I half rose and Crawford, without saying anything, pulled me down again beside him. Then I thought of the proximity of the petrol tanks and wanted even more to get up and go. Then it stopped. We had passed over that particular battery. As with the onset of a storm there is an intermittent spotting of rain before the deluge proper, so now there was only a sporadic tapping of tracer fire before we ran into the barrage proper. We were flying relatively low and gradually descending to the dropping height of 800ft. We were within easy reach of the ground, over which we were moving at a speed of not more than 120mph on a steady course, in broad daylight. We were a plum target, which we all realized. What we did not realize was that the enemy was waiting for us, with a newly amassed variety of anti-aircraft weapons, all along the last part of the route of the fly-in.

Presently the CO gave the order to stand in file and we got up and stood one behind the other, ready in an instant to hurl ourselves through the door like a crowd of passengers pouring out onto a platform. Over the shoulders of Colonel Lea and his batman I could see straight through the door and on to the ground, which now seemed very close indeed. Other Dakotas in the formation lay in easy view, rising and falling rhythmically on the invisible respirations of the afternoon thermal, their markings standing out clearly in the fine afternoon light. Near the door were the unlit red and green signal lights, the former expected to flash on at any moment in preparation for the jump. All at once a cluster of dirty black smoke puffs appeared about fifty yards away, followed a fraction of a second later by a harsh tattoo of explosions which drummed across the sky, a succession of very loud metallic sounds like a nose-to-tail pile-up of vehicles on the MI. Soon the whole sky seemed to be sprouting black puffs and reverberating with metallic explosions, the view through the door at one time becoming obscured by dirty splodges, like the windscreen of a car following another through splashing mud, and it seemed impossible for any of us to remain unscathed.

As though in a dream I saw a black puff appear immediately below an adjacent Dakota and one of the supply containers, which was slung like a large bomb from the bottom of the fuselage, become detached at one end, swing awry and fall off. Then another nearby aircraft started to bank slowly out of formation, dragging a wing with dirty yellow flames and black smoke trailing from the engine, and with horrible inevitability spiralled slowly earthwards. I could imagine all too clearly the scene inside; imprisoned paratroopers waiting like ourselves for the order to jump, while the pilot fought to keep height and on course. It was already too late, half way to the ground before men appeared, jettisoning themselves with hopelessly slow precision. The first dozen or so parachutes opened, the last few had no time, and as the Dakota hit the ground and burst into flames a man was still framed in the doorway. I noticed the red light flick on but could not have been more alerted and ready to jump than now, for it was requiring all my will-power to control an overwhelming desire to push past the two men in front of me and escape into the air.

A sudden explosion louder than the rest caused the Dakota, already plunging unsteadily through the turbulent air, to lurch violently to one side, to buck as if going over a hump-back bridge and to deposit me and some others unceremoniously back on our seats. I noticed through my window the port aileron had been shot away and the trailing edge of the wing was flapping like a line of washing. As I recovered myself I also noticed a large jagged hole high up in the side of the fuselage and another in the roof where a shell fragment had passed through.

There was now an accelerated urgency in the desire of each man to get out of the plane, which spread like a fuse through the stick, those at the rear pressing upon those in front, crowding up on Colonel Lea who stood, half crouched like a sprinter before the door, with his arms stretched out against either side of it and his fingers gripping outwards round the edges, ready to pull himself out on the instant the light went from red to green. He, feeling the growing pressure from behind, turned his head over his right shoulder and looked down the stick. His face was grey and beads of perspiration stood on his forehead and trickled down the side of his eyes, but his expression was firm and completely composed.

'Stand steady there,' he commanded clearly. 'Stand steady.'

The well modulated voice carried, even above the noise of the engines and bursting shells, to the furthest man in the stick. Its tone had a scolding quality, as if he were at pains to show disappointment at having to say anything at all, but it also contained the strength that sustains when it is needed most, the conviction of the resolute that a surrender to fear is a surrender to the will of the enemy, and that battle is first and foremost a conflict of the spirit; and the men in the stick stood steady, while the plane that carried them plunged through the barrage, piloted by men with the same ancestry in their blood, whose dedication to their task was even more complete since their destiny lay irrevocably with the plane, from which they would never have time to escape.

I wondered if anyone had been injured by the shell but could do nothing as my business now was to get onto the ground. Any minor wounds incurred in the plane I would treat down there, while a casualty unable to jump would be treated by the despatcher. The noise of shell bursts and the bucketing of the Dakota intensified as the river Neder-Rhine came into view, and I could see flak barges moored along the northern bank, winking incandescent spurts of fire at us as we passed over. I saw another Dakota bank sharply out of the formation and slide sinisterly downwards out of sight. We were very nearly there. I noticed in quick succession a railway line and a wood then, a fraction of a second later, saw the green light come on, heard the despatcher shout, 'Go,' saw Colonel Lea disappear into the void, his batman already half out of the door, and found myself battling with the force of the slipstream with his head just below my feet. I involuntarily shut my eyes while I waited for the powerful tug on my shoulders which is the glorious reward of the jump. Then there was a blessed silence.

I looked up gratefully at the canopy billowing above my head and experienced a feeling of relief second to none in my whole life. I was out of the Dakota and had survived a terrible danger. But I was oscillating violently on the end of the parachute and my first action, after unstrapping the kit-bag from my leg and lowering it to the end of the line, was to manipulate the rigging-lines in such a way as to steady my descent. That done, I took a quick look round, trying to pick out Dwyer and Adams from the cluster of parachutes of which I was the centre. But all looked alike in their camouflage smocks and crash helmets and I was unable to see a Red Cross armband. Then I looked down quickly because, although after leaving the plane there had been an immediate healing contrast of quiet, I could now again hear the sound of explosions, and I looked in horror as the piece of ground on which I was shortly to land erupted all over in tulips of black smoke.

'Oh, my God,' I found myself shouting out loud, 'they're shelling the DZ.'

I began frantically to search the ground, now rushing up at me with increasing speed, in the hope of finding a safe place to land. I had started to oscillate again and, although paralysed by a feeling that every German in the vicinity must have his gun levelled at me, the habit of training asserted itself and I became absorbed in the technical business of making a safe landing. I was drifting backwards and still swinging. If it can be timed so that the last backward swing just clears the ground, the forward swing that follows may cancel the drift and landing backwards may sometimes be no more acrobatic or difficult than stepping off an escalator. As it was, I contrived just to clear the ground on my last forward swing so that I both swung and fell backwards, failed to roll properly, struck the back of my head stunningly on the ground and had the knock-out completed by the Red Cross haversack bucking off my chest and hitting me on the jaw and mouth.

I lay completely dazed, not even aware that I was being dragged along on my back by the parachute that was behaving like a spinnaker in the wind. When at last, perhaps after several minutes, I had come to my senses and gathered my wits sufficiently to realize my predicament, I started struggling desperately to collapse the canopy and disengage myself. In a fever I smashed at the safety catch to release it, and then tried to roll onto my face so that the 'chute could be blown off my back, but being festooned with so much equipment I could not manage it, and somehow I had to struggle to my feet and collapse the canopy by pulling on the rigging lines before it came free. I started to run blindly towards the nearest man I could see and was immediately thrown heavily to the ground again by the kit-bag, which I had completely forgotten, and the line of which had become entangled round my legs. Cursing, panting and sweating, I laboured to undo the kit-bag and extract the rucksack, all the time conscious of the firing and prickling with a sense of danger.

When at last I had got my arms through the loops and humped it onto my back, I sank, exhausted by the struggle, onto one knee and, pushing the helmet on to the back of my head, wiped the sweat off my forehead with a sleeve and took a quick look round. The view was not encouraging, most of it obscured by a heavy smoke pall through which the rays of the sun occasionally slanted like yellow searchlights. There were no longer any aircraft or parachutes in the sky, I could smell the acrid tang of cordite and of burning vegetation, and hear the crump of nearby explosions. There was not a single Allied soldier in sight and I felt near to panic, like wanting to burrow frantically into the earth, anything to find safety.

But, as the seconds passed and nothing worse seemed to happen, reason began to assert itself and I started to try to think constructively in terms of finding the Battalion rendezvous. None of the landmarks, which had been memorized so carefully from the air photographs, were identifiable. The dropping zone was a kind of sandy heath, carpeted with heather and surrounded by woods, but in one corner, the south-east, there was supposed to be a culvert under a road bridge where the CO had decided to set up his first command post, and where I was to rally with my medical section.

I fumbled with a pouch in the webbing and pulled out my compass. South-east. The smoke now had cleared somewhat and over in that direction I could see a rise in the ground and beyond it some trees. The rendezvous must be there somewhere. It had to be there. I started to run, at first scrambling along, crouched over, doubled up to make myself as small a target as possible; but the weight of the rucksack soon began to make my back and shoulders ache and, before long, I had to straighten up. On doing so I found I could see over the rise and, with a flood of relief and joy, a small group of our men, in the midst of whom was Major Dan Webber, all facing alertly towards the wood, which now appeared a mere hundred yards or so away. I shouted and he turned motioning vigorously to me to get down. I raced the last few yards and flung myself down, choking with gladness, beside him.

'Oh Dan, am I glad to see you –' I began.

But he interrupted me with a forefinger to his lips and spoke into the walkie-talkie apparatus he had been operating. 'Starshine here. Message received and understood. Out.'

'Now, Dan,' I went on, 'can you now tell me what in hell's name is happening?'

He was brief. 'No time, Doc. We've got to get going.' Rising to his feet as he spoke, he motioned the men to advance. 'Keep spread out,' he ordered, 'and you'd better drop back a bit, Doc. Keep me well in sight and do just as I do.'

'You bet I'll keep you in sight,' I acknowledged fervently.

We advanced steadily towards the wood, and every now and then I heard the swish of something passing rapidly through the heather. I did not realize at first what was causing it until I connected it with firing that was coming from the wood, and then I started to walk on tip-toe, like a ballet dancer, until I was struck by the sheer futility of it and settled back on my heels. I could now see that the edges of the dropping zone were alive with men, all going roughly in the same direction as ourselves and, by the time we reached the wood, the noise of firing had abated very considerably; and we stopped in the undergrowth while once again Webber operated the walkie-talkie... It was not long before he switched off with a grin all over his face.

'It's OK. The Battalion's secured the rendezvous. We will advance in single file along the edge of this wood. Lieutenant Bishop is acting as rendezvous marker. When you see his moustache you'll know you're there.'

Lieutenant Bishop, whose handlebar moustache was an outstanding feature, had dropped the day before with an advance party whose mission was to take and hold, if possible, both the rendezvous and the dropping zone until the Battalion's arrival.

As the men gathered themselves up and started to form into file, Webber rapidly put me in the picture. Bishop's advance party had had no difficulty in taking the dropping zone and rendezvous yesterday, but had been hard put to hold it today. The Germans had counter-attacked with a company or so with machine guns and mortars, and it had been these that had greeted us on our arrival. But they had soon withdrawn when they had seen the scale of our landing, leaving a few sharp-shooters in the woods. It was these Webber and his men had been going after; but the CO had given the order to ignore them and join him.

My spirits quickly began to rise. This was better. If, to mix my metaphors, the dropping zone had seemed like Dante's Inferno, the meet up with Webber was Paradise Regained. I looked at my watch, not quite twenty minutes past two, incredible to think it was such a short time ago that we had heard the first shot fired, when in the Dakota.

As we marched in single file, along the sandy track by the edge of the wood, the air was resinous with the smell of firs and pines, and I was aware it was a beautiful September afternoon and I was very hot. I was also aware that my mouth was swollen and one of my front teeth was missing as a result of the blow I had received from the haversack on landing. I palpated the haversack for a hard object. The culprit was a bottle of brandy, euphemistically known as the medical comfort. 'A bit hard,' I thought, and then laughed at my own joke. I was certainly feeling more like myself.

Smoke had cleared from the heath on our right and there was a jeep in the middle of it, with a small party frantically loading the contents of a container, one of the hundreds which had been dropped by parachute among the men. The presence of the jeep meant that the gliders must have arrived in force. It also confirmed that the opposition encountered on landing, despite my own experience, had been quickly overcome. It would, in fact, have been surprising if a brigade of men, highly trained in the business of fighting on these terms, had not been able to deal with a company or so of the enemy, who must have been overawed at the sight of the huge force dropping on them out of the skies. But I had been dazed by the events, had received shock after unexpected shock from the moment when the aircraft, contrary to expectation, first ran into the barrage. The baptism of fire had been abrupt and shattering and, in the noise and confusion with which I was beset on landing, it had seemed miraculous that anybody could have known what to do, and that order could have been so quickly brought out of the apparent chaos.

Very soon the path brought us to the rendezvous. There was the road bridge under which it passed, and there stood Bishop agitating his moustache and waving us to come on. A little to one side, where the road continued after crossing over the path, there was a clearing in the wood round the edge of which were parked several jeeps. The clearing was thick with men, and the air noisy with shouts of command as they sorted themselves out into their fighting formations. Somewhat apart was a group of forty or more Germans standing sullenly with their hands on their heads. Apart from these Germans the whole scene had the air of a well-rehearsed exercise such as had often been performed at home; indeed there was no reason why it should not since there were no enemy now attempting to interfere. Bishop, who wore a piece of parachute silk knotted carelessly round his neck, clapped me on the back as we passed.

'What ho, Doc! Last as usual,' he said. 'Work's been pilin' up while you've been loiterin' out there. Deucedly unpunctual the lot of you, if I may say so. Carry on under the bridge and report to the CO.'

I made a rude sign at him and he feigned shocked surprise.

Under the bridge Colonel Lea and the group that constituted his headquarters were rapidly breathing a cohesive life into the Battalion which, having been partitioned into small but self-sufficient segments for the purpose of the air-lift, now needed reforming into an effective fighting unity. The vital arteries of the Battalion's existence were the lines of communication between Lea and his Company Commanders, which now hummed with wireless signals. An orderly was at the same time receiving messages from Brigade Headquarters and handing them to Lea, who was in earnest conversation with his second-in-command over a sheaf of maps spread out on the bonnet of a jeep run in under the bridge. Coming up to them I noticed a blood-stained field dressing applied to the right hand of Major Lonsdale who, catching sight of me, straightened up and beckoning said, 'Ah, Doc. The man I've been wanting.

Take a look at this will you. I got a scratch in the plane but this bloody dressing's getting in my way. Put something smaller on, sticking plaster or something, so I can use the thing.'

I started to undo the dressing, to treat my first battle casualty. To grind away at medical books, while Spitfires battled with bombers overhead, had seemed an intolerably inappropriate task during student days in London. To treat soldiers' feet, inspect latrines and kitchens and dispense stomach medicines had not, apart from the fact that I was in uniform, seemed very much better. This was more like it, what I had been preparing for.

As I worked Lonsdale continued to study his map. The last turn came off, stickily, and I held on tighter to his wrist. The little finger was lacerated and furrowed to the bone which, with a narrow strip of skin, seemed to be the only tissue left joining it to the hand.

'How did you say you got this, sir?' I asked.

'Oh, I don't know,' said Lonsdale irritably. 'Bullet or shell splinter or something. The plane was hit several times.'

'You ought to have it repaired properly.'

'Properly! What do you mean properly. Can't you do it, Doc?'

'No. Not here. You'll need to go to the Dressing Station and let one of the surgeons do it.' I hesitated. 'It ought also to be splinted.'

The major exploded. 'Damn and blast it. I can't go messing about with Dressing Stations and splints. It's only a scratch. Put something on it for the time being and I'll try and get along there later.'

I hesitated again. 'You may lose the finger, sir.'

'My God, Doc. Stop flapping around like a wet hen. Bind the blasted thing up now and make me serviceable.'

I complied. Richard Lonsdale was a professional soldier, a veteran of the Tunisian and Sicilian airborne operations, who knew the business of fighting battles of this kind probably as well as anyone in the Division of his rank. It was no time for text-book niceties. To try to persuade him to regard his wound from a medical point of view was as useless as passing a bottle of milk round a sergeants' mess.

'By the way,' he addressed me again, 'your Medical Sergeant's got some casualties through on the other side of the bridge. Will you form a temporary RAP* there, so I can let the companies know where you are.'

I moved to go.

* Regimental Aid Post.

'But don't unpack,' he added, 'we shan't be staying long.'

I saluted and squeezed through the knot of men in the direction Lonsdale had indicated. The sandy track, emerging from under the bridge, wound on across a clearing into another part of the same wood it had previously skirted. Just under cover of the trees a Red Cross flag hung from a branch, and beneath it half a dozen or so men lay on the ground. A man on a stretcher was being loaded onto a jeep specially rigged with a framework over the bonnet to carry it. Sergeant Dwyer was kneeling beside one of the wounded, while Adams stood to one side, writing with a stub of pencil on a casualty card against the trunk of a tree. I dropped quietly onto one knee beside Dwyer.

'What have we got here?'

Dwyer started. 'Sir! So you made it OK. Adams and I have been wondering what happened to you.'

'I've been wondering the same about you. Where'd you get to, Adams? Never saw you on the DZ.'

Adams, who had squatted down beside us, wore a look of concern. 'I'm sorry, sir. I landed near the CO and as you weren't anywhere about I followed him.'

I looked at the wounded man on the ground. 'What about this chap? What's his trouble?'

'He's been shot in the shoulder, sir,' Dwyer volunteered. 'Machine-gun bullet on the DZ. I've put on a field dressing. He's not bleeding now and is next on the list for transfer to the DS.'

The man on the ground was following us hungrily with his eyes as we talked. I patted him on his other shoulder.

'You'll be OK,' I said. 'Just take it easy and don't try to move your arm.'

We went round and examined the other wounded men in turn, Adams with two pencil stubs, one behind each ear, to write up the field cards. They were all casualties of the landing, except one who, like Lonsdale, had been hit in the plane by a fragment of flak. They seemed more surprised about their wounds than hurt, and one looked unbelievingly at his splinted leg and asked if he would be able to walk again. Dwyer took it upon himself to answer. ' 'Course you will, mate. Ever heard of anyone in the army doing anything else?'

It was reassurance that was wanted, as much as the morphia or hot tea that would be awaiting them at the Dressing Station, where they were shortly to go. I wished we could do more for them, but our job was simply to administer first aid. The Battalion would be moving on as soon as it was sorted out, at any time now, and, prompted by Dwyer, we made a tally of our equipment and I sent a runner to contact the medical sections with each of the other companies for a report on their battle readiness.

I sat down near the Red Cross flag and leaned back against a tree. I found I was a trifle weary after all the excitement, but with the ebb of immediate danger my composure and confidence had returned. Now, with the support of my Sergeant and the apparent order that reigned I felt myself once again a secure cog in the well-oiled airborne machine, a condition certainly preferable to the precarious independence experienced on the dropping zone. Dwyer was supervising the evacuation of the wounded to the Dressing Station. They had to be driven on jeeps about three quarters of a mile back down the sandy track beside the wood, along which I had come with Webber, to a large country villa where the Dressing Station had been established. In an airborne division a Station carried its own operating and intensive care teams, all brought down in gliders with their equipment – containers or personal haversacks – and it was able up to a point to function as a hospital.

There was apparently no shortage of transport and the work proceeded quickly. Soon word came in from the companies that the medical corporals and stretcher-bearers were present and correct with their full quota of equipment, all the wounded had been evacuated and we were sitting about on the ground rather aimlessly. As time went by and we made no move, I began to feel restless. I got abruptly to my feet.

'Keep an eye on things, Sergeant. I'm going to see if I can get some gen.'

As I made my way back towards the bridge I passed several groups of men who invariably asked me the same question, 'How's the exercise going, sir?' And I as invariably replied, 'Fine. A piece of cake,' and it was too – now. Although I had this feeling in my bones that we ought to have been on our way to Arnhem instead of sitting about in the sun. Over at Battalion Headquarters I found Webber peering intently at the mechanism of his Sten gun.

'What's up?' I said.

'Sand,' he replied.

'No. I meant what's up with the exercise. Why are we still here?'

Webber continued to fiddle with the mechanism of his gun.

'Signal trouble.'

I waited for him to go on.

'So what?'

'So we're still here.'

Signal trouble might be no joke. It was not the moment for back-chat. So I said, 'Anything serious?'

And then he told me. There had been difficulty in raising Divisional Headquarters on the wireless sets for a start. When our brigade, the 4th, had finally established contact it was to learn that the battle plan had had to be changed. The 1st Brigade, dropped yesterday, had run into unexpected trouble. One battalion alone had managed to get through to the Bridge but the others had been held up. Instead of our battalion making for the north of Arnhem to form part of a screen against enemy counter-attacks on the Bridge from that direction, it now had to make straight for the Bridge itself to try to link up with, and reinforce, the battalion holding it. We had been assigned a new route into Arnhem, the last part along the north bank and in sight of the river Neder-Rhine – the low road as it became known.

I looked at this new route as Webber pointed it out on his map, between five and six miles, all of this to be covered on foot. Assuming there was no serious opposition it could be done in three or at the most four hours, but it was now more than an hour since the landing. In exercises at home seldom more than quarter of an hour was spent in organizing a move off after the drop. It was apparent the time schedule was getting into arrears, first the take-off delayed by fog, then dealing with the opposition on the dropping zone, and now the signals trouble and new planning. According to the original plan the Division was supposed to have occupied all its final objectives by nightfall today. Now it would be getting dark before we could be in the outskirts of Arnhem. I voiced my disquiet to Webber.

'We were told there weren't supposed to be any enemy troops in these parts except lines of communication and the odd ulcer battalion.'

'Well, seems there are. Intelligence probably boobed. But don't worry, Doc. Monty's expected up from the south tomorrow and we're down in strength. They won't be able to stop us.'

As I walked back to my aid post I saw in my mind's eye the vision of our full strength moving into Arnhem. Apart from the probing and flanking patrols, the main body of the 11th Battalion would use good roads wherever possible to facilitate the passage of the jeeps, guns, motor cycles, cycles and hand-carts which constituted its wheeled transport. It would advance in a long column extending for more than a mile, and the medical section would be very close to the rear all the way so that we could always catch up and overtake casualties and not have to retrace our steps for them. Behind the Battalion would come the Field Ambulance, alias the Dressing Station, with their fleet of ambulance jeeps.

A whistle blew and was echoed by others deep in the tracks and woods, which suddenly became alive as hundreds of recumbent or seated figures rose to their feet and hastily refastened belts and buckles loosened for comfort. The Headquarters at the bridge had been the centre of Battalion activity, but all around had been watchful men facing outwards, some half a mile from where my section and those in our immediate vicinity had been able to relax in comparative safety. We followed a track through the woods to begin with and, just as the rear elements were moving off from the rendezvous area, there came the growling sound of rapidly approaching low-flying aircraft.

'Some more of our famous air cover, I expect,' said Sergeant Dwyer. 'Sound like Typhoons to me.'

I looked up. 'Almost certain to be.'

But almost before the words were out of my mouth I hurled myself to the ground, shouting, 'Get down. For God's sake get down. They're Jerries!'

As they roared over their machine guns started spitting, and I felt my flesh creep all along my back to the nape of my neck and the roots of my hair. Then suddenly they had gone and all was silent again.

'Blimey,' exclaimed Adams, 'you still there, sir? How many were there?'

'I only saw three,' I answered clambering shakily to my feet, 'but that'll do for the moment.'

There were no casualties from this little episode and I felt rather foolish, suspecting I had misjudged the danger and overreacted. It would have been more dignified, and probably much safer, to have knelt quickly behind a tree placing it between myself and the line of fire, than to have grovelled, shouting, on the ground. It was the newness of it that was the trouble.

Now we were marching on silently through the woods, our feet raising a fine cloud of sand, the sun glancing through the autumn foliage in muted tones of gold that dappled on our camouflaged helmets and smocks, by which we merged remarkably with our surroundings. The sound of shuffling feet and grinding gears was punctuated by the harsh cry of blackbirds as they flew away in alarm from these strange looking invaders of their peaceful territory. Sergeant Dwyer, small of stature, looking like a bunched up mushroom under his rucksack, marched warily, darting his head this way and that as though he expected to find a German hiding behind every tree. Two of the men in the medical section were pulling along collapsible handcarts piled high with gear, another was wheeling a folding bicycle with stretchers strapped along the cross-bar. Behind was my jeep which had come in one of the gliders and joined us at the rendezvous, stacked with panniers, stretchers and haversacks.

At one point we came out of the woods onto a piece of partly ploughed and cultivated open country, much smaller than that onto which we had parachuted, which was crammed with an impressive jigsaw of gliders, many of them lying wing-tip to wing-tip as though marshalled there by a car park attendant. The tail of the bigger gliders had been jettisoned by an explosive charge to simplify unloading, and lay angulated to one side like a useless fractured limb. Tracked Bren-gun carriers and jeep-drawn anti-tank guns would have been driven out of the bodies of the gliders at top speed. I wished I could have seen the landing, a cloud of these amazing monsters wheeling out of the sky like vultures, no sooner on the ground than their striped bodies erupting with men and metal. Some of them were tilted with tails in the air. Their wheels would have sunk further and further into the soft ploughed earth until buried and arrested, and any momentum left in the glider would have thrown it on its nose. The landing speed however was relatively slow and those in them mostly escaped with a severe shaking unless it turned completely on its back. In one place there was a glider partially consumed by fire and still smoking, but there was no sign of its crew, dead or alive, so presumably it had been fired after landing.

I had never had any desire to go by glider, it always seemed a far more hazardous mode of delivery than by parachute. For the glider pilots one could have nothing but admiration. Beginning as soldiers they then trained furiously to obtain their pilot's wings with the one object in view of landing in some enemy-held field. Having achieved it they reverted once again to soldiers and fought beside the men they had flown to battle. Their airborne life was as brief and delirious as the love flight of a male bee; only they were far from spent and useless on their return to earth, their regiment being one of the most redoubtable in the Airborne army.

After going steadily for twenty minutes we found ourselves beside a railway line on our right which, according to the map, carried the main line traffic between Arnhem and Utrecht, the same line we had seen from the plane just before the jump. We kept to the north side of it for another half-mile, while all the time a house visible from afar off became more and more distinct, and presently revealed itself to be the home of a level-crossing keeper who, with his wife and family, stood in their front garden cheering and waving and offering cups of water to the exuberant troops. At the house we turned right and crossed the railway and almost at once found ourselves in the small village of Wolfheze.

Here the inhabitants had turned out in force to line the main street, and the scene that I had until now only read about in the newspapers and seen on the newsreels was repeated with an intensity that equalled anything I had been led to expect. While the faces of the younger women and children were bursting with smiles and cheers and laughter, those of many of the older people were furrowed with tears. The road was strewn with trampled flowers, and dogs and little children ran beside the column uttering their own brands of shrill welcome. They pressed upon us cups of water and rosy apples which we were thankful to accept, and everywhere the Churchill 'V' sign was used as a currency of friendship and greeting. They would grasp and shake us by the hand, while now and then a girl would run and plant a kiss on a soldier's sweat-stained cheek. Their joy was spontaneous and uninhibited, and their trust and confidence obviously whole-hearted and unreserved. So much so, that they gave me, and no doubt every British soldier who passed that way, a renewed vigour and confidence in ourselves and our enterprise, and a fresh impetus to succeed. We had not encountered a single German since leaving the dropping zone, and morale was sky-high.

We kept on through the village, until some way beyond, again in the open country, we halted. I lit a cigarette and took a look at the map. We must be approaching the junction of our road with that of the main road from Utrecht to Arnhem, along which part of our route lay. I beckoned Dwyer over and asked him if he had heard anything filtering down from the front companies. All the time we marched, especially since we had got onto better roads, members of the Provost section had been motoring up and down, keeping the convoy of men in their correct stations, and there had been numerous opportunities for an exchange of information with them. The eyes of the Battalion were the patrols out in front and their view of things was very different indeed from that of our medical section, marching quite blindly like the rear legs of a centipede, knowing nothing of what was going on further up, only that which swam successively within range of our own senses. If the Battalion had halted there must be a reason. I could see a lot of men in front, a handful immediately behind and wooded country to either side.

Even as I pondered we started to move on again. From this point onwards our progress became slower and slower, punctuated by ever more frequent halts, until it soon became obvious we had no hope of reaching the Arnhem Bridge before nightfall. I supposed the forward patrols were finding the going more difficult as the country gave way to the built-up suburbs of the town, with large villa-like detached houses set in good-sized gardens on either side of the main road. They had to make sure these houses did not conceal the enemy who, by holding their fire, could surprise and disrupt the main body of the Battalion as it passed through.

We did not see many civilians now; an occasional group would stand and wave at a garden gate, but as dusk approached the gardens became deserted and the houses shuttered. We marched in a double file, one on each side of the road, in alternating groups, under cover of an avenue of trees. During one of the halts I thought I could hear firing in the distance, and Dwyer and Adams and I sat by the roadside straining our ears in the direction of Arnhem, which now lay only some three miles or so ahead. The next time we stopped there was no mistake about it, and as the darkness deepened flashes could be seen in the sky. There was a rigid black-out in Holland and only a very occasional chink of light escaped from the shuttered houses. There was no moon and visibility was very bad – so bad, in fact, that from time to time when passing beneath a particularly dense patch of tree-foliage we were obliged to keep contact with the man in front by putting a hand on his back. Occasionally a man would wander off the road and find himself tripping over uneven hillocks of grass or running into trees. If we had been following a sandy track, as earlier, it would have been very difficult going indeed, but the feel of our boots on the hard highway helped to keep us on course. We were in a fully built-up area when total darkness fell, and orders were received to reduce all noise to an absolute minimum. It was an eerie sound we made as we advanced in the dark, made up of rasping boots, rattling equipment and the subdued throb of jeep engines. It might have been unwelcome to any German who was listening, but heartening to a Dutchman identifying it with liberation and the fulfilment of his hopes.

Despite the difficulty of maintaining station and keeping contact the darkness was an advantage, in that it gave us a chance to penetrate deeply towards our objective without the precise knowledge of the enemy, who could only guess at our presence and strength from the clues of sound. On the other hand it meant we might also march into a prepared trap if the enemy had any foreknowledge of our intentions. It depended which side of the coin one liked to look at. Whatever lay in store, we had to press on. Our very role necessitated the burning of our bridges. We were trained and expected to fight on our own without open lines of communication with a base. As we saw it, relief for us could only come over Arnhem Bridge, we therefore continued on into the darkness, feeling our way down the road. A very slow, tiring and nerve-straining business in the deep blackness of the night.

At one point we arrived at a crossroad where we turned off to the right down a minor road that led towards the river, passing on the corner to our left a large hotel-restaurant which dominated the crossing. There was a good deal of light showing from this building, and my interest quickened as I saw ambulance jeeps parked at the entrance and a bustle of activity around them. From one of the jeep drivers I learned that the glider-borne Field Ambulance, landed yesterday, had established itself there as a Dressing Station, and already had many wounded on its hands resulting from the two days of action.

The road, now much narrower, was lined by houses on the hotel side and trees on our right, and went downhill gradually towards the river. There were outbursts of fire from the Bridge area and, every now and again, a dancing glimmer like summer lightning would illuminate the sky away in the distant south where the main liberation army was grinding its way towards us. Apart from the intermittent firing there was nothing to be heard except our own scuffle and rattle, we spoke little and then only in forced whispers. The air had become very chilly, and every time we stopped and rested by the wayside I had increasing difficulty in resisting the temptation to lie down and sleep. Progress began to resemble the uncertain, spasmodic jerkings of a run-down clockwork toy. We would go a short way and stop, teeter about on our feet or sit down, and then set ourselves in uneasy motion again, the tail of the column belatedly reflecting the movements of the forward elements, who were nosing and probing and feeling their way slowly but surely down the dark, menacing road.

After several hours of agonizingly slow progress in this manner, during which we had drawn close to the river following its northern bank, we passed under a railway line. This line was carried over the river by a girder bridge and had been one of the subsidiary objectives of the 1st Brigade. It was too dark to make out the bridge but I knew we had now reached a point not more than twenty or thirty minutes march from the main objective. Almost at once we halted again, and this time the word came back down the line that the Battalion would stay in this position until daylight, and fall out by the side of the road taking what cover was available.

It was one of those occasions when it was an advantage to be in the Medical Corps, because being non-combatants we were not required to take part in guard-mounting. The section found itself halted by a house with a moderately sized front garden into which it dispersed itself. Most of the garden was given up to the growing of food, and I found it impossible to select a bed for the night that did not entail at least partly lying on cabbages or parsnips. As I was divesting myself of equipment Dwyer reported briefly that he had put a Red Cross flag on the garden gate, and detailed one of our men to sleep near it, so that if any casualties were brought in we could all be quickly roused. He added he had heard the Battalion was going to put in an attack as early as possible in the morning.

Adams and I, after eating some concentrated food and drinking a little water, lay side by side under the wall of the house, our bodies wrapped in waterproof capes and our heads on haversacks. I wound my wrist watch. The luminous hands stood at five past two. It had been a long day.

I must have fallen straight to sleep, for the next thing I was aware of was a penetrating chill in all my limbs, which were stiffened and cramped with cold. I glanced at the watch and saw it was now three twenty-five. I sat up and in the darkness groped for my waterproof cape, which was no longer properly around me, and after rearranging it lay with my back close up against Adams, who slept on unperturbed by such minor discomforts. I lay thinking of the night I

43

had spent sleeping in a slit trench which I had dug myself on the Yorkshire moors during an exercise and which became half full of water as it poured down endlessly in a cold, drenching rain. Even then I had managed to sleep some of the time and now, once again, I dozed off into an uneasy slumber, content to let my thoughts drift while my body rested.

Tuesday 19 September

When I next awoke properly it was to find myself in a grey, misty world full of strange noises. It was intensely cold, and I got quickly to my feet and started to stamp about and fling my arms around my body to restore circulation. There was a cock crowing away to the north, somewhere behind the house, and the sound of revving jeep engines on the road. It was half past five, the same as yesterday only far from the same. Yet Adams and Dwyer had risen before me, as was their wont, and at that very moment Adams emerged from the front door of the house carrying two large mugs of tea in one hand and a kettle in the other.

'Good morning, sir. Char's up,' he announced with a satisfied grin. 'Now, if you will let me have some of your oatmeal I'll fix some porridge.'

I took the tea gratefully and handed him my haversack. Dwyer then came over to join us from the garden gate where he had been standing.

'Sergeant,' I said reproachfully, 'wish you had woken me sooner. What's the gen?'

'Sorry, sir, didn't seem much point. Get all the kip you can's my motto. Nothing's happening.'

An occasional shot from a distance was punctuating our conversation.

'What's that, then?' I asked.

'Sniper, so they tell me, from somewhere over there.' He pointed up the slopes behind the house, which was now revealed as one of a row of two-storey dwellings, here and there scarred by marks in evidence of some kind of engagement yesterday or the day before.

'I've been up to Company and all they could say was we were to stand by and be ready to move. They seem to be waiting for the CO to get back from Brigade.'

I lit a cigarette and held it in my lips, while brushing the vegetable garden debris off my battle-dress and re-attaching all the various bits of equipment to my person. Adams handed me a mess tin full of the concoction of oatmeal. I was grateful for the hot food. It is wonderful what it will do on a cold grey morning to summon up strength and morale. After partaking I felt quite chirpy and strolled round the section, chatting to the men and enquiring after their well-being. Most of them had passed a fitful night but had been asleep more often than not. From the time they had last wakened in England they had been on the go for the best part of twenty hours before they finally halted for the night, and now it was only a few hours later with a long day of unknown stresses in front of them. But they were all young, some of them very young: nineteen, twenty, twenty-one, and they were fit and strong as they would probably never be again for the rest of their lives.

In the improving light the river could be glimpsed, away on the other side of the road behind a large factory with a tall chimney-stack at one end. The railway, after running southwards over the road bridge which we had passed under last night, continued along a high embankment to the river, where it terminated abruptly in the smashed girders and collapsed arch of the river bridge, which must have been blown up by the Germans before the 1st Brigade had a chance to take it. The road towards our objective was lined by Airborne men waiting and facing expectantly forward, while a queue of jeeps lay nose to tail with the drivers already in their seats and the engines ticking over. We were all at present in dead ground, protected by the houses from the slopes behind us. Apart from a few discreet rifle shots there was absolutely no sign of the enemy. The air was fresh, the morning was beginning to sparkle and all the men looked jaunty and confident. A kind of watchful intentness for the first sight or sound that would proclaim the imminent test of their martial prowess now settled over this keen, battle-eager assembly. Sure of themselves, sure of each other, their comradeship bound together with a quick bright thread of pure steel, they were a crack unit, knew it and enjoyed the knowledge. They had a reputation as fighters which, because they had made it themselves, seemed to assure their destiny.

I had not seen a casualty since leaving the rendezvous and was lulled by this non-event into a feeling of immunity. I felt the worst was over. Maybe a battle was about to develop, but I just could not anticipate it as something that might result in men dying or flesh being torn from bodies, certainly not from mine. I was a non-combatant. Why should I be harmed? I can now only ascribe this blatant over-confidence and lack of realism to immaturity, coupled with an inherently escapist side to my nature. But what of the others? Might they not to some extent feel the same. Would wars be fought at all if everybody concerned had seriously to write themselves off before it could begin?

I was set down on a small road in a strange country, for all the world like the rear wagon of a large goods train. Provided the links held, I would inevitably move forward when the whole train moved, or backward as the case may be, but I would know little or nothing of the track over which I was to travel until I came to it. I depended on others entirely for information, not being supplied with a walkie-talkie or other wireless communication, and would know only what my superiors chose to tell me or what I took steps to find out. Now, out of direct verbal touch with any other officer, the world had contracted into the brief horizon of my unaided eyes and ears. My job was simply to be there, ready to treat casualties. All that really mattered was that the company commanders should always know my position, so that the wounded could be brought or directed to me in their need. I would, therefore, send a runner forward from time to time to keep Headquarters informed of my exact whereabouts, and from this runner I hoped in turn to derive whatever information was available.

The next few hours were a repetition of the previous night. We advanced in fits and starts with innumerable halts, keeping to the pavements and not making much attempt to seek cover. The jeeps proceeded up the crown of the road. There was more and more fire from in front, but it sounded far away from where I was and it might still have been an exercise in England. The trees, which abounded among the houses, were heavy with autumn foliage, yet retained a prominent hue of green. Only an occasional, furtive face behind an incredibly clean window betokened the presence of the Dutch. On the sills colourful plants grew from a profusion of pots, while the trim gardens proclaimed the care recently lavished upon them and somehow emphasized the predicament of their owners, who no longer appeared alfresco as they had done yesterday at Wolfheze.

Gradually, imperceptibly, like London traffic in the early morning, the noise increased. The now more than occasional crack of rifle fire was augmented by the deeper bark of Bren guns and other automatic weapons, while the movements of the men became increasingly stealthy and swift. When they stopped, they slipped into gardens and drives and lay behind gate posts and shrubs, their weapons pointing up the road. They would dart forward, quick as prawns in a pool, and then melt into the background.

Sergeant Dwyer, Adams and I were thus lying side by side in a garden, when a loud crack and the whine of a ricochet caused us to duck our heads down very quickly.

'My God. That sounded close,' I muttered. 'Where the hell did it come from?'

'Not sure. From the left I think.'

'Let's find a better spot than this.' I looked about me. 'There. Up by that wall. Come on.'

We rose together and ran, doubled up, to flop once more onto our stomachs and lie uneasily on the dank earth, stirring up the sharp odour of newly fallen leaves.

'They seem to be having a little difficulty ahead by the sound of it,' said Dwyer, 'and look,' his voice took on a note of excitement, 'there's a bloke being carried back on a stretcher.' He raised himself for a better view and then gripped me by the arm.

'That would be a better place than this,' he said, pointing at a short concrete drive between two closely set houses a little way on, leading directly to the garages belonging to them and flanked on each side by a garden wall.

I took a good look. 'I agree. Let's get the section in there and open up shop. It will give us cover from all sides except the road.'

Dwyer shouted for the section to follow and we all dashed up the road, and swerved into the drive like rabbits. Adams draped the Red Cross flag over the open gate, where it could be seen from up the road, and waved at the stretcher bearers, who were coming steadily toward us.

'In here, quickly chum,' he shouted. 'Set him down careful. Now then – name, number,' and he busily set about writing down the particulars it was his duty to record.

The man had been hit in the leg, but it was a flesh wound already covered with a field dressing and, as the bleeding seemed to be staunched, I contented myself with giving him a shot of morphia and a few words of encouragement.

'That doesn't look too bad. How did you get it?'

'They got me and one or two others with a burst, when we were crossing the road,' answered the man, almost apologetically.

He was from one of the forward companies, and the stretcher orderlies who had brought him said there were some walking wounded making their own way back as well. The Germans had been sniping at them regularly and there had been a machine gun mounted in a house that had taken them by surprise.

It was now nine o'clock. For another three quarters of an hour there was little shooting in our immediate vicinity, but plenty further on, and the Battalion did not seem to be making any progress. Three walking wounded arrived; two with superficial wounds but the third with a smashed arm, which I splinted and put in a sling. The jeeps were still strung out along the road with reserves of ammunition and weapons. From time to time odd bodies of men, not from the Battalion, would pass along towards the noise of battle. General Urquhart, the Divisional Commander, himself came by in a jeep, which he stopped when he saw the Red Cross flag, and leaning out enquired how everything was. His strong, bluff, heavily moustached face was mostly hidden by the low-rimmed helmet and its chin-strap, but I was held by his eyes, roving everywhere, constantly moving as he awaited my reply, taking in my set-up one instant, gazing up the road and then back over his shoulder the next. He seemed possessed by a sense of urgency but spoke without haste. I saluted him and answered, lamely, 'Under control, I think, sir.'

He gave me a penetrating stare which made me feel quite uncomfortable, then added, quite informally, 'In case you don't know, although I expect you do, there's a CCP* recently set up a quarter of a mile back.'

'Thank you, sir. Good luck, sir.'

He acknowledged with a smile and, giving us the thumbs-up sign, ordered his driver to proceed. I felt enormously cheered. Things must be all right if the General was here in person; but no sooner had I savoured this thought than there was a sharp recrudescence of firing, sounding much closer than before, and another whining ricochet made us all crouch down in a hurry. Almost at once a soldier appeared, supported by two others, limping painfully up the drive, and all three ducked as another shot rang out. The realization quickly grew that we would need more cover and more room to carry out the work properly. The little drive was becoming crowded and did not seem as safe as it had before. The rifle cracks came

*Casualty Clearing Post.

regularly from somewhere up the slopes behind the garages. The jeep drivers were taking cover behind their vehicles and the road, apart from them, appeared deserted. Across the other side of it I could see a soldier wedged in a doorway scanning the slopes, and closer scrutiny revealed the presence of others behind garden walls and fences. I beckoned one of the medical orderlies and ordered him briefly to go back and try to locate the CCP the General had mentioned.

'Tell the officer there I've got some casualties and would like them evacuated as soon as possible. Come straight back with a jeep yourself if they've got one to spare.'

The orderly saluted and disappeared. I turned to Dwyer. 'Look, we'll have to get these wounded men into the garage so that they're right under cover.'

'I've already tried the door and it's locked,' Dwyer replied, and then suggested, 'What about going into the house itself? That would be better still.'

I had not thought of that. 'You may have something there, Sergeant,' I mused.

He went on, 'We could use the garage as a kind of waiting room for those waiting evacuation and for the less seriously wounded, and take those needing treatment into the house. We could have a nice brew-up too.'

'Sounds OK. But I don't want to get us all settled in there just as the Battalion moves on again.'

'If you ask me, sir, doesn't look much like it at present. We seem pinned down good and proper.'

I considered a moment before answering. 'There can be no harm in taking a look. Anyway I'll have to ask them for the key to the garage. Keep an eye on things. I'm going in.'

There was a small gate by the garage that opened onto a path leading to a side door of the house. I went up, rang the bell and gave a rat-tat-tat on the knocker. The door, after a short pause, was opened by a studious looking man in glasses, wearing a dark suit and white collar. He looked to be in his early thirties and said earnestly, before I had time to speak, 'Good morning. You want water? The washroom is through here.'

I glimpsed two women standing further in behind him and said, 'Good morning,' adding as I crossed the threshold, 'It would be better if we shut the door.'

The Dutchman stepped aside, closing the door after me, and then, as I passed in front of the women, said, 'This is my wife and mother.'

We shook hands in turn, myself solemnly saying, 'How do you do,' and apologizing for my dirty hands.

'I would be very glad of a wash, thank you.'

'This way then.'

He led the way to a downstairs lavatory, of which I gladly availed myself. As I washed I was thinking, 'Everything is so terribly clean. Can't bring the section in here, we would make such an awful mess.' Inside the house the firing seemed far away and irrelevant, and I decided to settle for the garage. When I emerged from the lavatory the Dutchman moved towards me.

'I see you are a doctor. I have watched you. My wife and I would like to help.'

I voiced a thought that had, oddly enough, only just struck me. 'You speak English very well.'

He nodded and smiled.

'I hope you are glad to see us.'

'Oh yes. Oh yes.' He grasped me by the hand again and shook it vigorously. 'Oh yes. But we are so worried. The Germans are so strong. Will it be victory, you think?'

'Of course it will,' I replied without hesitation. 'We're only held up temporarily. We shall be advancing again soon, and we expect the liberation army in from the south today or tomorrow.'

I really believed it as I said it, and not only because I felt such sympathy for the Dutch, who had had this battle dropped upon them.

'I really came to ask you if we could borrow your garage for our wounded. They will be taken away soon but, until they are, it would be quieter and safer for them than out in the open, where they are at present.'

'Oh yes. I see. Well of course. I'll unlock it for you.'

His wife, to whom he spoke a few words, disappeared for a moment and then returned with the key. He then accompanied me down to the garage which was stacked high with a miscellany of domestic articles, including a sewing machine, pram, bicycle and collapsible canoe. He never hesitated.

'We use it as a store. The things can just as well go in the garden.'

With these words he started carrying the articles out of the garage, through the gate leading from the drive, and piling them on the lawn behind the house. With the help of the medical section the garage was soon cleared, and as the last item was deposited on the lawn he came up to me and said, touchingly, 'Is there anything else we can do for you?'

'No, thank you, we can manage now. It would be better for you and your family to stay in the house until the Germans are pushed out. It won't be long.'

'Do you think we should remain in the cellar?' he asked anxiously.

'It would be safer as long as there is firing. I will let you know when we move on so you can get your things back in the garage.'

'Thank you,' he said turning to go, 'indeed we are glad you have come. It has been terrible these past years – terrible. This is nothing. Good-bye for now.'

When he had disappeared Sergeant Dwyer turned on me with a note of disappointment in his voice. 'The house, sir, what about the house?'

I explained my feelings on the subject. 'I didn't feel we could, for the short time we are likely to be here. You never saw anything so clean and there are a couple of women in there. We can't drag them into it. Anyway it's much better now we've got the garage.'

The orderlies began moving the wounded, those unable to walk, who lay on their stretchers quietly and patiently, saying nothing but intently watching every movement of the RAMC men. There was no more to be done for them at this stage, until the bearers from the Clearing Post came to take them back, en route for one of the surgical teams at the Dressing Station who would examine their wounds under an anaesthetic, and carry out the necessary detailed treatment. My concern, having taken the immediate measures required for the saving of life and limb, arrest of haemorrhage, combating of shock, relief of pain and the prevention of further damage through movement or infection, was now to see them safely off my hands to where the really skilled treatment was available; that mending and repair work which determines the outcome, not only from the point of view of life but also from that of appearance and later usefulness.

The firing further up the road came in short angry bursts, lasting a few minutes and then subsiding to a background noise of intermittent popping. Every now and then would come that shot from much closer which seemed to be searching especially for us, and was quite clearly delivered by a sniper who had our particular section of road under observation. In the immediate lee of the garage I felt secure and, having taken station there, did not mark the arrival of a jeep bearing Red Crosses until a shout, 'Hallo. Mawson?' brought me out running.

'Lawson, you old so and so. Fancy seeing you! Come on out of the road. It's not safe.'

The arrival was the medical officer in charge of the Clearing Post, who had worked in conjunction with me on several exercises and was about my age. We shook each other's hands vigorously, and he clapped me on the shoulder.

'I got your message. So here I am with your orderly. I've set up the CCP in a barn, you can't miss it, about five hundred yards back on the side of the road away from the river, but I'm out of touch with my Field Ambulance. I thought I'd come up with the jeep and see what's happening.'

'Not much I'm afraid, old lad. We've been stuck here some time and, as you see, there have been some casualties. None serious but one or two need surgery.'

'I've quite a lot in the barn. The chaps on the high road have caught it a bit. The 1st Brigade Field Ambulance is in the Elizabeth Hospital not far forward of here. I think perhaps I ought to go to try to contact them. I'd like to arrange to bring up my CCP casualties to them when your lot moves on.'

'Sounds a good idea. But for God's sake be careful. It's pretty hot in that direction. Jerry's got automatic weapons trained on the road. But you ought to make it. The General went through not long ago.'

'OK. I'll go on foot. You use the jeep to get your wounded back to the barn. My sergeant's there, he'll look after them. I'll try to get back and find you as soon as I can. OK?'

'OK. But wait, old man. Stay and have a brew.' I offered him a cigarette. 'Adams will get you one in a jiffy.'

Adams had, in fact, once the wounded had been moved into the garage, busied himself with a portable stove which was now delivering uncertain spurts of flame to the bottom of a small iron cauldron. Making tea at all hours had become ingrained into the pattern of his life. He faced abnormal situations by the reassuring performance of a familiar rite, thus divesting the moment of its abnormality and reducing it to terms he could understand and manage.

Lawson declined the offer of tea, saying he had partaken just before leaving the barn, but accepted the cigarette and, after taking a few puffs, adjusted it in the corner of his mouth, shook me again by the hand and set off cautiously up the road. I watched him until he disappeared round a bend that swung to the left about eighty yards further on, and then returned to the garage. Dwyer, who had been privy to our conversation, was checking the labels tied to the wounded, written by Adams, that detailed the wound, the time it was received and the treatment given.

'They're ready to move, sir,' he said. 'Shall I get them cracking?'

'Yes please. Right away.'

'Bearers,' said Dwyer briskly, 'first two stretcher cases on the jeep. Look sharp now.'

The wounded on stretchers had been laid in the garage in a line of order of priority for evacuation, and the first jeep load was quickly completed and sent on its way. Adams, having eventually coaxed the cauldron to boil, produced a hot liquid which passed for tea and, when the remaining wounded had received their share, the medical section partook of this refreshment while awaiting the return of the jeep. I opened a conversation. 'We've got quite a cosy billet here don't you think, Sergeant? And with this nice cup of tea it feels quite like home.'

'Home seems a long way away to me just now,' said Adams. 'I wonder what they are doing back at barracks.'

'Depends on what the time is.'

I never forgot that brief exchange because it marked the end of all my thoughts of the action as an exercise or game. It was a bridge of words that led from a relatively bright landscape, where the architecture conformed to accepted rules and events were still understandable and manageable, to an abrupt, dark kind of nether region where to grope about in apprehension and bewilderment became the new pattern of existence; where the future was quite unpredictable, the past unreal, and the present, because of the jagged uncertainty of life, became a single pin-point of nerve-tight awareness. For it was eleven o'clock, and at that hour precisely the Germans mounted a counter-attack that seemed to break up the Battalion.

There was a whistle and a very loud crash, harsh and metallic like the sound of cars in collision, followed rapidly by others in the near vicinity. I stood momentarily, mug of tea in hand, stunned by the unexpectedness of it, then headed, tea and all, for the ground. After a few trembling seconds I raised my head from its ostrich-like position beneath my hands, which I had clasped over the back of my neck, and looked up the drive towards the gate. Nothing seemed to have altered and I said to Dwyer, who had dropped to the ground beside me and was now getting to his feet, 'What the hell's all that?'

'Mortars I would say.'

'Theirs or ours?' I queried fatuously.

'It's a sizeable Jerry attack by the sound of it, and coming this way. I'd better take a look.'

'Be careful,' I warned, 'it sounds damn close.'

Dwyer slipped out of the garage and edged his way to the gate as the crashes continued. He dropped flat and looked cautiously round the post, then beckoned to me. I repeated his manoeuvre.

'Look, sir, it's falling up there where the road bends.'

I looked where he indicated, horrified and fascinated. There was a heavy pall of smoke hanging over the road and gardens, and a litter of broken pavé and branches. A man would dash, doubled up, across the road or out of one of the gardens into another and, as he did so, there would be staccato bursts of automatic fire. A jeep came backing out of the smoke, and outside our gate the drivers were lying on the ground beside their parked vehicles, cautiously watching the scene ahead.

At this moment the Red Cross jeep reappeared from the other direction, being driven slowly by an obviously anxious driver. I cupped my hands and shouted, 'Quick. Back her in. It's all right here.'

It was a matter of seconds only before the jeep was off the road and into the drive.

'Well done. What's it like back at the CCP?'

'It's quiet, sir,' replied the driver in a surprised voice. 'Nothing happening at all. You run into this lot quite suddenly.'

'OK. That's fine. We'll get all the wounded away from here as soon as we can. Let's see how many we can get on the jeep this time.'

We managed to load all but one of the remaining stretcher cases on to the jeep which then set off again, with its somewhat precariously balanced cargo, for the barn. I instructed the walking wounded to follow it and make their own way there, and told Sergeant Dwyer to get all the gear packed and place the section in a state of readiness to move. I then lay down again by the gate and peered round the gate post trying to make up my mind what to do for the best. The mortaring was getting on my nerves. If it came any closer, I told myself, our position would become untenable as a refuge for the wounded. At the same time I half expected to see more casualties appearing down the road, and they did at least, at present, know where to find me. I might have to put my aid post in the house after all. It would be safer but then, if the Germans were to succeed in their attack, we could well be overrun and put in the bag. What I really needed was information. I beckoned Dwyer to join me and told him what I was thinking.

'You could send one of the orderlies up to investigate,' he suggested. 'My guess is they're holding casualties in the houses for the time being, or sending them to the Elizabeth Hospital. It's only just round the corner isn't it?'

I pondered. I needed to know what was happening but I did not fancy the chances of anybody trying to get through to wherever Webber happened to be, and back again. I certainly would not have fancied them for myself. Where in the hell was Dan Webber, where Colonel Lea or Major Lonsdale, where in the hell, in fact, was there another officer? The smell of cordite had drifted down the road, an unappetizing seasoning to an already indigestible meal, and I began to feel physically sick as my mind went round in an unhappy whirl of indecision. I knew Dwyer was waiting for me to give a lead, and that the section were depending on me to take the right line of action. Unfortunately I too had been used to dependency on senior officers and, at this juncture, I felt I needed more than anything to have an example to follow in the handling of myself and my men, in this immediate and relentless danger.

As it happened the impasse was suddenly broken by the unexpected diversion of seeing two Airborne men jinking back past the gate, followed quickly by others, and then by a jeep.

'They're retiring, sir,' shouted Dwyer.

His shout jerked me out of myself and brought me to my feet. Before I realized what I was doing, I, too, was shouting and running out into the road towards the driver of another jeep in the process of reversing.

'Where the hell is everyone going? What are you doing?'

'We're ordered back out of range, sir,' came the reply, flung hastily into the bedlam of noise.

'Then, by God, we'd better go too,' I thought, and bolted back to the garage gesticulating and again shouting, 'Come on, Sergeant, all after me. Bearers pick up that stretcher. At the double.'

It took a very few minutes to gather up the equipment, and for two bearers to take up the remaining stretcher and wounded man. Even so, I sweated uncomfortably for what seemed an age before we got on the move. There was a house burning furiously fifty yards up the road, and the windows of those all round were cracked or broken. Loose tiles, paving stones and empty ammunition cases littered the ground, while the branches of trees hung in shreds, the white wood poking through the bark, like bones through skin, where they were fractured. There was a trickle of men emerging singly or in small groups from the holocaust, like animals escaping from a forest fire, dodging and weaving through the gardens, dropping and rising with the whistles and crashes of the mortars.

The jeeps had disappeared from view when we began our sprint or what was in effect a fast trot, and it could not have been more than four or five minutes after Adams plucked the Red Cross flag off the gate before we found ourselves well away from the bursts and in comparative quietness. I had re-sighted the jeeps parked in line by a row of houses, that had no gardens and abutted directly on to the road and, out of breath and shaking, I called a halt. As soon as the two orderlies who had carried the stretcher put it to the ground, they collapsed like rowers after a boat-race. There was no sign of another officer anywhere, but there was a Corporal standing in a doorway with a Sten gun under his arm, and a cigarette in his mouth. As I approached him he did not change his stance.

'Where are you from?' I asked sharply.

'Headquarter Company,' he replied, without taking the cigarette out of his mouth.

I felt savage. 'Take that cigarette out of your mouth and address me as sir. Have you seen Major Webber and do you know where he is?'

The Corporal removed the cigarette and held it cupped in his left hand; straightening up a trifle, he looked at me rather malevolently.

'No. Sir. He was some way in front last time I heard of him. We were the rear section.'

'Who gave you orders to retire?'

'No one. Me and my section dodged into a house when the Jerry started on us and when we saw the jeeps moving we thought it time to scarpa.'

'You received no definite orders, then?' I pursued.

'No, sir, no orders. There was no one to give us any in our house. We just thought, when the jeeps started back, that a retirement was on and we'd better get with it.'

'OK, Corporal. At ease.'

As it seemed the backward movement of the jeeps was the precipitating factor in this apparently unscripted drift in the wrong direction, I made haste to question a jeep driver. He was quite cheerful and simply said they had been told to move the jeeps out of range of the mortars.

'Who told you?' I pressed him wearily.

'Company Sergeant Major, sir,' he replied.

'Go on.'

'He sent another driver back, whose jeep had had it, to tell us. Said we'd to keep the jeeps intact whatever happened, and he'd send a runner on a bicycle when he wanted us up again.'

'Where's that other driver?'

He pointed him out and Dwyer, having ranged the medical section along the north side of the road under the lee of the houses and stationed himself at my elbow, peremptorily called him over; but he was unable to shed much further light on the course of events. He said he had been attached to Company Headquarters and, when the mortaring started, they, HQ, had gone into a house. He'd stayed in the road with the jeep until it was hit and then gone into the house, too. He said Major Webber had gone on ahead to contact the CO, leaving the CSM in charge. The CSM had ordered the jeeps back and he was told to go with them. He had just run like hell and hoped for the best. He knew nothing of the whereabouts of the company stretcher bearers.

One thing I was not used to, and had not foreseen, was this feeling of isolation from the chain of command which normally controlled every aspect of my service life. Apparently, I was the only officer in the immediate area and was being cornered, by force of circumstance, into assuming responsibility for half a dozen or more jeeps, carrying a load of vital ammunition, and a group of fighting men, even now augmented by others who appeared in view retiring uncertainly down the road. Among them was a Sergeant whom I singled out, asking him the same clockwork question: 'What's happening? What's going on?' But the Sergeant could not throw much light on the scene either.

'Things look bad, sir,' he said. 'There's all merry hell let loose up there. They've got Spandaus firing on the road from up the hill, and are plastering it with mortars as well. The Battalion's in a bad jam, they've got us pinned down in the houses and got all the windows covered. You can't see where they're firing from and if you show yourself you've had it.'

'No chance of advance, then?'

'No chance at present. On the other hand they'll have hell's own job winkling us out of the houses.'

'And the wounded. What of them?' I supposed there must have been some casualties.

'We've not been able to move them out of the houses.' I thought, 'My God, the whole thing's going to pot,' but said to the Sergeant, 'Have you any idea what's supposed to happen next?'

'I understand we're trying to disengage and reform,' he replied. 'The CSM assumed control of HQ Company after Major Webber went forward saying that was the plan.'

'Are there any other officers you know of in this sector?' I was getting apprehensive.

'Not that I know of.' The Sergeant was emphatic.

I tried to force myself to think calmly. It certainly did not seem proper to me that our fighting men should be retiring, so apparently haphazardly, from their vital objective without orders from HQ, and without a clear-cut battle plan. Even if they were all pinned down in houses some walkie-talkies must be working, every platoon had got them. I sensed the Sergeant and the others were waiting for me to take a lead. There appeared to be no immediate threat from the Germans where we were now. The noise of battle, although not far distant, was like a fire-engine hastening through the next street compelling all to listen, but not alarming because not directly approaching. I ceased being a doctor for a few moments and tried on the mantle of tactitian.

'Sergeant. These men will come under your command and you will take up a strong defensive position here. If the Battalion is disengaging it will need a firm rear. There must be no further withdrawal. The jeeps may move if necessary, but (we were on a minor crossroads) this is a good position and we must hold it.'

'Yes, sir,' said the Sergeant doubtfully. 'But we're very short of ammo, sir.'

I felt a rising impatience. 'Well, good God man, get some more from a jeep or something. You don't suppose the medical section's got any?'

'No, sir,' said the Sergeant with what my senses received as exaggerated deference. 'What positions do you suggest we occupy?'

I grew more impatient still: primarily with myself for the incompetence I felt to deal adequately with the situation and, secondly, with the Sergeant for expecting me, a doctor, to know the answer to such a question. I stifled the retort born of irritation and said instead, 'I'm sure you know that as well as I do, Sergeant. Use your own judgement and proceed as fast as possible.'

With these words I turned away to bring the interview to an end. I did not want to be asked any more questions to which I did not know the answer. It was enough to have to decide where my own medical section should now be positioned. 'Hell,' I thought, 'what to do now? Get into a house or stay in the open? If I put the section in a house the cover will be better, but in holing up we run the risk, as before, of being isolated and put in the bag. On the other hand, if we stay in the open, we may get caught in mortar fire.' The whole position seemed so unstable there was no absolute rational answer. I was not only irked by my ignorance of the overall picture regarding the position of the Battalion, but face to face with my inexperience of battle conditions and how best to cope with them.

In the end I elected, on instinct, to remain in the open and voiced my decision to Dwyer. 'I propose remaining in the best open cover we can find near the road, so that for the time being we can be ready to move immediately, and keep an eye on what's happening up there.' Dwyer pulled his mouth over to one side and screwed up his eyes.

'I would have preferred to have been in a house, sir, it's a luxury we never had in the desert.'

Not having been in action in the Western Desert or anywhere else until now, I felt he had the advantage of me and inwardly began to waver, but held on to my chosen course.

'Well, supposing there weren't any houses round here, where would you choose to site the RAP?'

Dwyer looked around him distastefully. 'Not much choice, sir.' He pointed back the way we had come, where a little lane ran to the left off the main Battalion road axis. 'Up there I should think, sir.'

It had a breast-high hedge and a small drainage ditch on each side and, by sitting on the side with our feet in the fortunately dry ditch, we could remain concealed and at the same time keep the battle-front under observation through gaps in the hedge. Adams spread the Red Cross flag over the hedge at its junction with the road, while Dwyer despatched one of the bearers some fifty yards up the lane to keep a watch on our left flank.

The day was wearing on and the sun becoming quite warm. There was an air of semi-rustic peace around the small area we occupied, making it difficult to believe that the devastation and shambles created by the mortar shells really existed such a relatively short distance away. But the noise was there all right and, perversely, I recognized I would be made more anxious by its stopping than by its present racketing, which at least served to mark exactly where the trouble and danger lay.

But we had not been there, basking in the sun, more than ten minutes when our peace, if it may be called such, was rudely and irrevocably shattered by a sudden crescendoing whistle and earth-shaking crash, which heralded the arrival of another mortar barrage with a pattern of fire seemingly centred on our very position. My first reaction was to jump to my feet and look around, but, on seeing the columns of smoke erupting everywhere, I hastily dived into the ditch and started grubbing and scrabbling my way under the hedge with my bare hands. I felt as if each whistle was seeking me out personally, and the bombardment of explosions was like the blows of a sledge-hammer against the imperfect resolution of my will, which threatened to crack as the minutes of fright accumulated. I lay in the ditch with my face buried in the leaves and my hands clasped over the back of my neck, flinching violently with each crash, and feeling utterly naked and exposed, gripped by a sickening, freezing fear that immobilized my body with invisible chains of ice.

Then my thoughts, which had been fleeing blindly down the corridors of my mind away from this unbearable reality, came to the unpenetrable wall of realization that death itself was very near and all around, and there was no such thing as personal immunity. In a desperate rejection of such finality I started mentally twisting and turning, like a fugitive in a cul-de-sac frenziedly seeking a means of escape, until I came to see that if there was to be any way out I had to charge through my pursuers. I could not just wait for them to get me. A sudden very close near-miss did it. My chains snapped and I found myself leaping to my feet, waving my arms about, and shouting wildly, 'Come on, Sergeant. Come on. The barn. The CCP. We must find the barn. All follow me.'

And with these words I ran blindly away down the road, not once casting my eyes behind me to see if Dwyer, Adams and the section were following. Yet very soon after the first few minutes of unthinking flight at my topmost speed, I began to be aware, as the tide of fear receded, of a left-over pool of shame until, by the time I eventually reached the barn, still not having looked back, it had become an ugly mark I did not like to contemplate.

The barn, easily discovered by the great Red Cross flags spread out on the roof, was approached by a short alleyway between a group of houses leading to a small cobble-stoned courtyard, on one side of which was the barn and on the other, the side of a house. The end was closed by a gate opening onto a cluster of small out-houses, beyond which a wooded slope dominated the scene.

I stood in the alleyway leaning against a wall struggling to gain composure, taking great lungfuls of air and fighting down a desire to be sick. The danger had now evaporated as suddenly as light is dispersed by the mere throwing of a switch. I had placed a few hundred yards between myself and the shell bursts; since I could now only distantly hear them, there seemed no longer any immediate danger to my person and fear fell from me like a cloak. But the bad taste remained. Should I not go back and make sure Dwyer, Adams and the section were safely on the way? The face-saving, ego-protecting process inherent in every human being took over. 'I'm too bloody exhausted to do anything at the moment,' I thought. 'Got to get me breath back. In any case they've wounded in here. Need a doctor. Can do more good here than back there lying on a butcher's slab. Told Dwyer to follow me. Knows where I am. Sure to find this place. Can't miss it. I'll go in and see what I can do.'

When the Sergeant, who had been left in charge of the barn, happened to look up from what he was doing to a blood-sodden mess on a stretcher and glance towards the barn door, he saw, striding in purposefully, a smiling, self-possessed British officer, about five foot eleven in height, fresh-faced but with a stubble of beard and a front tooth missing, who, although dusty and dirty and out of breath, still had the remains of sharp creases in his battle-dress trousers and an immaculate knot in his tie; and the officer, after pausing for a moment and casting his eyes round the scene, spotted him and, coming over, said casually, 'I'm Captain Mawson, RMO 11th Battalion. Is there anything I can do? My section is only just down the road and on their way here now. My battalion is temporarily held up, and we might as well amalgamate with you for the time being.'

The Sergeant, unable to salute because of what was in his hands, drew himself to attention. 'I thought at first you were my MO, Captain Lawson, but I'm very glad to see you, sir. We've a lot of wounded here on our hands as you can see; some of them very bad. We're gradually getting them back to the DS. They're running a jeep shuttle service.'

'Surely not the one at the Elizabeth Hospital where Captain Lawson was making for?' I asked.

'No, sir, the glider-borne back on the Oosterbeek crossroads.'

'Where's that?'

'You follow the road back along the river till you come to a church then turn up right. About a mile and a half in all I should say, perhaps a bit more.'

'Oh yes, I remember seeing it last night. In a sort of hotel.'

'That's it.' The Sergeant paused. 'We're very short-handed here. Can use your section. If it wasn't for the Dutch nurse . . .'

'Dutch nurse,' I interjected. 'Dutch nurse. What Dutch nurse? Where?'

The Sergeant indicated a corner of the barn, and I made out a slight figure in an overall and white head-cloth kneeling beside a stretcher.

'How long has she been here?' I asked in astonishment.

'Since early this morning, sir. Just appeared. Said she could wash and feed the wounded. Captain Lawson tried to send her away, said it might be dangerous, but she took no notice. Just helped herself to some lint and water and started to sponge their faces.'

'Does she speak English?'

'Oh yes. Very well.'

My curiosity about the girl was interrupted by an orderly who, including me in his glance, reported a wound in need of attention as having re-started to bleed. I followed him, leaving the Sergeant with his original case, stepping between the stretchers which lay in four rows down the centre of the barn and lined every available space against the walls. The barn was full of men yet it was strangely peaceful and silent, the noise of the mortars sounding distant and unconnected, until suddenly the double doors of the barn were flung open and a jeep, driven in full pelt, brought with it all the raucous noise of the exploding world outside. It seemed sacrilegious, as if a taxi-load of revellers had driven down the aisle of St Paul's cathedral during mattins. I was aghast, thinking for a moment it was the enemy, but an area round the entrance had been kept clear and no sooner was the jeep inside than it was quickly loaded up with wounded.

The orderly, seeing the look on my face, said, 'We've had to bring the jeeps in, sir. Jerry started sniping at us when we were loading them up outside in the yard.'

'I see.'

The work of loading the jeep was soon completed and then, while the doors of the barn, shut as soon as the jeep had come in, were again held open, the driver let the clutch in with a jerk and accelerated out of the barn, tyres squealing on the cobbles, as he threw the jeep sharply into the turn needed to take it down the alleyway to the main road.

'We've had to keep the doors shut, not only because of the noise,' the orderly went on complainingly, 'but because at one time shots were actually coming in here.'

'I can hardly believe that,' I said, 'they must be able to see the Red Crosses.'

'It's true, sir.'

'Bloody Huns,' I thought. 'They must know this is a non-combatant unit.' Strangely enough this petty sniping that made necessary the repeated intrusion of the jeeps made me feel very angry. Outside with the Battalion the RAMC might not be very conspicuous. It could be difficult in the heat of battle for any German to notice a Red Cross armband, or even the small flag that marked the aid post. But here in the barn with the huge Red Crosses on the roof, put there for recognition by aircraft, and the equally large flags round the entrance, it was intolerable, a flagrant breach of the Geneva Convention. The anger and indignation did me good. To hell with the Germans, we'd beat them yet.

The wounded man to whom the orderly led me was the one the Dutch girl was tending. She had a large gauze swab in one hand, pressing it onto the blood-soaked bandages covering the man's thigh, and with her other she was stroking his forehead. His eyes were closed and the skin of his face grey and damp. There was a pool of blood under his leg. The girl looked up as I arrived. She was clear-eyed and fair, with a youthful, intelligent face and, although appearing outwardly calm, her forehead was puckered into furrows of anxiety.

I said, as I began to take the bandage off the soldier's leg, 'It is very good of you to come and help us but you should not be here, it is not safe.'

She smiled rather wanly. 'I think it is safer in here than it is outside.'

I conceded she had a point there, as it echoed my own sentiments, but I still could not get over the incongruity of her presence among us. I was on the point of remonstrating again but she anticipated me by saying, with great simplicity and dignity, 'Why should I not be here? Your men have been wounded for my country. I am glad to be able to help them. In any case,' she softened the force of her words with another smile, 'this is Holland, where I belong.'

There was no gainsaying her, nor the respect and admiration her attitude was arousing in me. All I could say, as the blood began to well up from the wound when the pressure of the bandage lessened, was, 'Thank you, nurse. Quick, more gauze.'

I snatched it from her hand, rolled it into a tight ball and jammed it hard into the depths of the now uncovered wound. In spite of this unavoidably painful treatment the man on the stretcher did not stir, and I looked at him anxiously.

'What's his pulse?'

'I'll take it.'

She set about it competently and quickly, timing it by a watch taken from a pocket of her overall.

'It is very difficult to feel, but I think it is about one hundred and forty beats a minute.'

I felt for the man's wrist with my spare hand. It was certainly very fast and very weak. I turned to the orderly. 'Get a tourniquet, quick as you can. He's lost a great deal of blood and is very shocked. And bring some water or tea, anything, and some brandy. We must try to get him to swallow some fluids.' I took some more gauze and stuffed it into the wound, pressing it with all the weight of my body on my fist.

'Do you know how much morphia he has had, nurse? It ought to be on his card.'

She scanned the label attached to his battle dress. 'Two injections of quarter of a grain each, the last twenty minutes ago.'

'Hm, that should be all right.'

When the tourniquet was properly in place above the wound, the bleeding lessened. I bound a field dressing over the gauze packs, and with the help of the nurse and the orderly propped him up and tried to force some brandy between his lips. It had a momentary effect. He fluttered his eyelids, made a few convulsive swallowing movements, coughed once or twice but never properly came to. I stood back and muttered to the orderly out of earshot of the patient, 'It's no good. He must have a transfusion or he'll die. We must get him to the Dressing Station on the next jeep. Absolute priority. Are there any more as bad as this?'

'I'm afraid there are, sir.'

'I'd better take a look at them. Nurse,' I turned back to the patient, 'you know about loosening the tourniquet?'

'Yes, Doctor.'

'Stay with him then will you, and let me know if you're in trouble.'

'Of course, Doctor.'

'Doctor, she called me,' I mused, following the orderly down the rows of stretchers to the next wounded man he wanted me to see. 'It's a long time since I heard that word.' It was, in fact, not since I was a very junior doctor at my London hospital. In the army I was always 'Doc' to the officers and 'sir' to all the other ranks. The girl's use of the word was at the same time a challenge and a balm to my self-respect. Damn it I *was* a doctor, perhaps not a very good one, but a doctor all the same, and that was why I was here in this place.

It was hot in the barn. Motes of dust danced in shafts of sunlight which slanted through paneless windows high in the brick walls. It was a short time past noon. I had divested myself of my equipment and camouflage smock, and was working with the battle-dress blouse sleeves rolled up to my elbows, passing from stretcher to stretcher examining a wound here, adjusting a dressing there, revising the order of evacuation as the condition of the wounded changed and the jeeps made their regular entry and exit. Always I was followed about by questioning, beseeching eyes in the grey faces of men who bore their sufferings silently and stoically. Adams was with me now, marking the casualty cards, for the section had arrived at the barn not long after myself. Dwyer had mustered the men out of the ditch, but their progress had been slowed by the stretcher case. I felt much relieved at seeing him and hearing his reassuring voice reporting the section all present and correct.

'Well done, Sergeant. It was rather a shambles back there.'

'I thought we'd had it, sir, no sort of place for the medics.'

'You'd better report to Captain Lawson's Staff Sergeant, there's plenty to do.'

Apparently Dwyer had not seen anything unusual in my precipitate departure, rather I sensed a sort of 'told you so' message from his demeanour and tone of voice. I had put them all in the ditch. Now, thank God, they were safely out of it. That I had ordered them out, however, could not expunge the self-knowledge that I had panicked and bolted. Soon they became absorbed into the work of the Clearing Post, preparing food, seeing to the needs of nature, carrying stretchers onto the jeeps and generally tending to the wounded, lighting cigarettes for them, feeding them, moving them when a position became too uncomfortable.

As time wore on the barn gradually emptied, until a stage was reached when, out of the sixty or so wounded men it held when I arrived, there were only five stretcher cases, twelve RAMC men, the

Dutch nurse and myself left inside. The noise of battle had been going on outside, waxing and waning, but, with all the work there was to do, one somehow was not too much aware of it. Not until one of the jeeps, as it came through the door, was followed by a vicious burst of small arms fire that brought all our heads up, as does a log falling from a grate and shattering sparks over a hearth.

The driver swore volubly. 'You'll 'ave to be bloody quick. The place is crawling with effing Jerries. I've been sniped at all along the road this end of the trip. It'll 'ave to be the last. The jeep can't be risked again, they're precious as gold. I've 'ad orders from the Field Ambulance.'

'You've actually had sight of the enemy?' I asked sharply.

'Yes, sir, flittin' among the 'ouses. They're all round 'ere and I reckon it won't be long before they're knockin' at yer door.'

My mind began racing. The evacuation must be finished, but it was obvious the driver's report on the feasibility of continuing, when he got back to the Dressing Station, was unlikely to result in his being sent back. My feelings for the preservation of the jeeps were nothing compared to the urgent necessity of getting the wounded and ourselves all out as soon as possible. An idea was forming: if I were to go to the DS myself and speak personally to the CO, I might be able to persuade him to send back enough vehicles at one time to empty the barn all in one go. Moreover, now that there was nothing left in the way of medical work for me to do here, I was getting anxious about the Battalion. Some of them, wounded, had found their way to the barn, which I had seen as serving as our aid post after the debacle in the ditch, but not for some time. I felt completely out of touch, and thought the DS might have some information enabling me to regain contact. Besides I had no desire to be put in the bag, which if the driver's report was correct, might be imminent. I decided to go on the jeep and take Dwyer and Adams. I outlined what I had in mind to the Staff Sergeant who had been left in charge of the CCP, telling him I was sorry to be leaving but it seemed the best chance of getting everybody out. Then I caught sight of the Dutch girl looking on anxiously, and on an impulse I said to her, 'Nurse, we believe the Germans may break in here at any minute. It really isn't safe now. Will you come with me to the Dressing Station. I'm sure there'll be more work for you there.'

She hesitated. I took her hand, led her to the jeep and helped her up. We put a stretcher on the bonnet on its special carrier and another on the back, then Dwyer and Adams and I piled in.

'OK,' I said to the driver, 'let's go, and fast.'

The barn doors were swung open, there was an abrupt assault of sound, the driver let the clutch in and, rapidly changing through the gears, accelerated down the alleyway and out on to the main road at a speed that would have meant certain death if we had collided with anything. He spun the wheel over into a right turn in the direction of Oosterbeek, and we would have all been flung out if not holding on to any and every available projection like grim death. As it was we were onto the opposite pavement and almost into some buildings before we came round on to the road proper, and really started to go. The stretchers were lashed securely and the wounded men strapped on, but the journey must have been a nightmare for them, lurching and bumping crazily as the jeep tore up the road. There was no time to gain more than a blurred impression of the scene. I was fully occupied in preventing the girl, round whose shoulder I had an arm, and myself from being shaken off. But I was aware of the sharp crackle of small arms fire all along the first few hundred yards, and instinctively kept my head down, fixing my eyes intently on the road ahead now strewn with the debris of battle as if a storm had passed, ripping slates, windows, chimneys and telephone wires and scattering them indiscriminately abroad. I saw no sign of life in this battle area but it was not entirely surprising. Men take the best cover they can in a contest of this kind, ensconcing themselves in buildings in which they may hold on until reduced to rubble.

Quite suddenly it seemed all the firing died away and the debris vanished. We found ourselves driving down an apparently peaceful country road, with meadows leading down to the river on our left and cultivated fields on our right. We passed a small church on the left and then, at a junction where we turned north away from the river, we were cheered by the sight of a group of Airborne men dug in with an anti-tank gun commanding the road along which we had just come.

'It's OK now, sir,' said the driver slowing up. 'We're in Div. HQ area. There's been no action of any kind round here yet.'

The leafy road, up which we now drove quite slowly, was indeed a peaceful contrast to the scene we had left. Birds could be heard chirping, and villas, now beginning to multiply, were bright with fresh paint and set in trim, well cared-for gardens. I realized what an incomplete impression I had gained of the place the night before, when groping down this same road in the dark. It really was very pretty, the woods gilded with early autumnal tints and the gardens still colourful with flowers. It seemed unbelievable that such a short way away the air was full of smoke and noise and the earth dese-crated by destruction and blood. In the last twenty-four hours the rapid alternations between danger and safety was an entirely new and unaccustomed pattern of life, to which I was not yet properly adapted: apprehension and calm, fear and relief. Events were forcing me to live more and more in the moment and at times, when one did not feel threatened, pleasure in simple things was immeasur-ably heightened.

Very shortly we arrived at the Arnhem–Utrecht road and domi-nating the crossroad, on our right, was the large hotel–restaurant, now visibly proclaiming itself as the Schoonoord, which had been occupied by the 181 Air Landing Field Ambulance as the already oft-mentioned Dressing Station. The road to Arnhem, down which other units of the Division had tried to fight their way, was a broad, cobbled boulevard, inset with tramlines and, in the village of Oosterbeek through which it passed at this point, lined by shops. If we had wanted to drive to Arnhem along it we would have had to turn right, cornering round the Schoonoord. A short way in the other direction, on the left hand side going towards Utrecht, was another hotel, the Hartenstein, taken over by General Urquhart as Divisional Headquarters.

The Schoonoord was a long low building of two storeys. Facing the Arnhem road, on either side of the main entrance, were large glass-fronted rooms normally in use as dining-room and bar-lounge. The dining-room had a separate entrance by way of two double-glass doors, and a short path, between the end of the dining-room and an adjoining petrol station, led to a service side-entrance. The jeep drew up at the forecourt of the bar-lounge, which was distinguished by a prominent stencilled notice marked 'Reception'. The forecourt in fine weather would have been occupied by tables and chairs and people taking their ease. Now it was peopled by wounded men on stretchers and the Medical Corps men moving among them. As our party began to climb off the jeep, we were approached by a tall, burly Major carrying a notebook and pencil in his hand.

'I'm Frazer. More from the CCP?' he queried. 'God knows where we shall put them.' Then, catching sight of the girl, he raised his eyebrows and added, 'Hallo, who have we got here?'

'A splendid nurse,' I said. 'She's been working in the CCP all day, but now it's getting too hot there, and I thought it best to bring her out. She wants to stay and help. She speaks perfect English.'

'Good show, the more the merrier. We've some others inside. And who are you and which unit are you from?'

'Mawson, 11th Battalion. Got isolated. Haven't seen them since this morning. It's pretty hot up in the town. We had to go back. I joined up with the CCP. They'd lost their officer, Lawson.'

'Lost! Do you mean he's been killed?'

'Not to my knowledge. I mean he's disappeared. He went up to make contact with the Elizabeth Hospital, but never came back. There are still three stretcher cases and ten RAMC personnel left in the CCP and if they aren't evacuated right away they'll be bagged. Three jeeps would do it if they're quick.'

'I know it's hot,' said the Major, 'the driver reported he's liable to lose the jeep. We need them all here. Sorry, dear boy, can't risk one let alone three.'

'Well in that case I'm afraid the chaps there will have had it.'

The Major's forehead puckered and he looked at me speculatively for a moment or two. 'Perhaps you had better see the CO,' I raised a 'who is he' signal with my eyebrows, 'Lt-Colonel Marrable, and put it to him.'

I followed the Major into reception where, in place of tables and chairs, the floor was covered, wall to wall, by wounded men lying on stretchers. We then passed on through into a large room which would have been the main hotel lounge, but which now had been transformed into the nearest approach to a hospital ward possible under the circumstances. Stretchers, not all occupied, lined the walls in place of beds, and on commandeered tables down the centre were laid dressings, antiseptics and other medical paraphernalia. In one corner stood a piano, and from the elaborately moulded ceiling hung a chandelier. Clean, well-groomed medical orderlies moved about their duties, and the absence of dirt was most noticeable after the dusty atmosphere of the barn. Leading off from this 'ward', through double doors towards the back of the premises, was another which, the Major informed me, was used as a resuscitation ward under command of the blood transfusion officer.

'We bring the ones that need to have operations out of reception into here, while those that need immediate transfusion go in there. We're using all the downstairs rooms and some of the upstairs as well. As you see, they're pouring in, more than we expected. There must be a hundred at least already.'

From the pre-operative treatment ward we went on through into the hall of the hotel. On the left was the reception counter behind which Colonel Marrable was ensconced, like a spider in the middle of his web. A staircase wound up behind the counter, and from this hall opened most of the downstairs rooms. Between the dining-room on the left and a small room opposite, now in use as the operating theatre, a corridor led away towards the kitchen and the side-entrance.

I saluted the CO, whom I did not know, not having had any connection with the glider-borne units of the RAMC. He was a calm, kindly looking man, probably in his early thirties, with well-brushed hair and immaculately turned out, who appraised me from behind a cloud of pipe tobacco smoke as I gave him a resumé of the situation in the barn and the need for jeeps. He let me say what I had to say without interruption and then, shifting his pipe to the other corner of his mouth, drawing on it and removing it, he commented incisively through the exhalation of smoke, that the driver had reported he could not do the trip again without great risk of losing a jeep they could ill spare. I said, very diffidently, 'There's an anti-tank unit at the church. Might it not be possible to post three jeeps in that area, where there is no sign of the enemy and they would not be at risk, and then send them up singly to the CCP to get the chaps out. It would not hazard more than one jeep at a time, and with a relay system like that and a bit of luck they could all be got out in quarter of an hour, I honestly think there's a good chance, sir.'

Marrable puffed away at his pipe and considered me intently. Then he turned to one of his staff. 'All right. Send three jeeps.' He then went into the details.

'Should I go with them, sir?' I was anxious to justify myself. Marrable shook his head. Frazer had introduced me and explained my circumstances.

'No. We must try and get in contact with your Battalion Headquarters and get you back to them.' Then addressing himself to a wireless operator, who was sitting behind him at a table on which was the set and a collection of message pads, he continued, 'Get on to Division and see if they can give me any news of the 11th. Tell them I've got their MO here who wants to reconnect with them.' He then looked distastefully at me. 'You might like to go up to my room and get a wash and a shave. Second floor, opposite the top of the stairs. You'll find some water in the wash basin. Leave your equipment there and come down when you're ready and we'll find you some grub.'

I climbed the stairs to his room and thankfully divested myself of my equipment. I stripped to the waist and taking toilet kit and towel from the haversack that had for so long reposed on my chest, revelled in the luxury of clean, albeit cold, water and the feeling of civilized security which it gave me.

The hands of my watch stood at half past two when, freshened and spruced up, I descended to the hall and presented myself to the Colonel, who had left his position behind the reception desk and was talking to Major Frazer. He looked up as I came down and took me by the arm in a friendly fashion. 'We've just been discussing what we had better do with you,' he said. 'Division has been out of touch with your battalion for some hours, and the ADMS thinks it would be better if you stayed here and helped us, at least for the time being. You will be glad to hear that the first jeep has got back from the CCP and the others are likely to follow. Go and have some food in the kitchen and then report to reception. You will be able to carry on looking after the casualties from the CCP there.'

In the kitchen I was handed a mess tin of stew, ladled out from a large cauldron standing on a range, and I wolfed it greedily, suddenly realizing how hungry I was. The catering arrangements in the larger medical units were often a matter for caustic comment and envy by others, who considered them somewhat pampered and feather-bedded. But the strength and resistance of the wounded had to be kept up, which entailed the provision of good nourishing food, and it was uneconomical of time and equipment for the cooks to serve different diets for patients and doctors. Participation in patient sustenance was, as it were, a professional perquisite.

Making my way to reception I noticed there were already fewer empty stretchers and fewer gaps on the floor of the pre-operative ward, and in reception itself there was scarcely room to move. Casualties had been coming in fast from units of the 4th Brigade who had been trying to fight their way into Arnhem, both along the main road outside the Schoonoord and a road north of the railway line. Extra buildings had had to be taken over, another hotel, the Tafelberg, on the opposite side of the road, where a surgical team was stationed, and a school. In the Schoonoord minor treatments and resuscitation were going apace, and in the emergency theatre amputations and other necessary surgical procedures were being carried out.

In reception itself there was scarcely room to move. The task was one of sorting: sorting out which patient was to go where for what treatment, and with what degree of urgency. At the same time there was the undoing of field dressings to examine wounds for these purposes, and the applying of others, while everything had to be properly documented with regard to decisions taken, drugs given at times stated, and wounds classified. Other medical officers were engaged in these tasks, which took longer than might be supposed because the crowded conditions gave us little elbow-room. Dwyer had been assigned to work outside, dealing with the constant inflow of new wounded arriving on jeeps or in commandeered cars or lorries, but Adams and the Dutch nurse were in reception and we got together and worked as a team. I made the examinations, Adams did the documentation and the nurse re-dressed the wound. Once this was accomplished, orderlies, under Major Frazer's direction (he was co-ordinating the whole work) carried them on their stretchers to their allotted destinations.

Now that I was safely shielded from the necessity of taking decisions, other than medical ones with which I was familiar, and was absorbed into the organization of a larger unit in a building whose own noises masked to a very great extent the distant noise of battle, I began to relax again into that deceptive feeling of immunity and imperviousness to unpleasant things. It might be thought the circumstances in reception were unpleasant enough, certainly they were for the wounded, and one might be accused of being callous if appearing unmoved by them. But a doctor's work brings him into contact with many situations of a harrowing kind, and the truth is the mind has a limited capacity for emotional drainage. There is a built-in mechanism that allows so much and no more, if one is to function at all effectively, and I think I must have already been drained by the events of the day. After the swift dissolution of all the ties, except for Dwyer and Adams, that identified me with my battalion, I felt I had been mercifully cast up upon a friendly and familiar shore.

We worked steadily through the afternoon and early evening. As it grew darker so it grew quieter, both outside and within, and, by the time we were relieved of our task at eight o'clock and called to have supper in the kitchen, the noise of battle had ceased. The walk through the hotel from reception gave evidence of all that the hard work had accomplished. All the lights were blazing and the wounded, looking clean and tidy, were lying neatly tucked into blankets with their equipment in a regular pile beside them. The floors were swept spotless and, but for the fact that stretchers and straw-filled palliasses were performing the office of beds, the atmosphere reproduced faithfully the hygienic orderliness of a military hospital. In the kitchen the Medical Officers were chatting informally with three other Dutch ladies, older than the nurse I had been associated with, although two of them were also of the same profession. The third lady was the owner of the hotel and of a temperament that must have been incomparably serene. At the very moment the Airborne army had dropped out of the skies on the first day, the hotel had been occupied by a high-ranking German officer and his staff, who had left in a hurry, and the next day it had been commandeered as a British Dressing Station. Yet, in spite of this treatment of her property, she was calm and smiling and unreservedly helpful, performing the most menial and distasteful tasks for the wounded, and setting an example of service that was an inspiration to all.

Towards the little Dutch nurse I was developing a feeling of proprietorship which became unexpectedly apparent when, after finishing her tea, she announced quietly, 'Well, I must go now.'

I thought at first she meant she was going back to do some more work for the wounded, and I begged her to sit down and rest a bit and have another cup of tea.

'No, thank you very much, all the same. I must go home.'

'Home!' I said incredulously. That she had a home somehow had not occurred to me. In fact I had not really troubled to think where she had come from. She was there when I arrived at the barn and had been 'there' unquestioningly ever since.

'But you might get shot or captured. It's dark and dangerous outside.' Then I added, 'Please don't go, nurse.'

She smiled. 'I think it will be all right. I do not live far away. My parents will be expecting me back. I will not get shot and it will be nothing to be captured. I have been a prisoner in my own country for four years already and I shall get away again as I did this morning.'

'You mean you'll come back here again tomorrow?' I asked doubtfully.

'Of course.'

She placed a hand reassuringly on my arm, stopped to say a few words to the proprietress of the hotel, and then walked out of the kitchen along the passage towards the service side-door. I went with her, following rather miserably at her heels like a dog, wondering what there was I still might do to dissuade her from going out into what patently to me seemed a very black and hostile night.

'Are you sure you're right to be going?' I asked lamely.

'Quite sure. Look out for me tomorrow.'

I stood at the door watching her as she walked out into the darkness, until I could see her no more. I suddenly felt very tired and thought I would go to the control point in the main hall where there were some arm chairs, and sit down for a while. Marrable was there, emanating calm, smoking his pipe and writing, and, beyond, in the pre-operation ward, one of the padres was doing his rounds and taking down letters at the dictation of those unable to write.

'Ah,' said Marrable, as I came into the hall, 'you've been hard at it all day, and I was about to send for you to suggest you try to get some sleep on my bed for the first part of the night. I'll wake you at two a.m. and then you can come down and be the duty officer here until reveille.'

'Thank you very much, sir.' I could not believe my luck. A real bed to sleep in. 'I'd be very glad to.'

'I should get off right away then, if I were you. It's likely to be another long hard day tomorrow.'

'Talking of tomorrow,' I hesitated, 'can you say how things are going? I've been thinking the Second Army must be nearly here by now.'

'So have we all. But I'm afraid the picture isn't clear yet. Communications have been very bad. We still hold the Bridge, that much I do know, but I fear your brigade did not come off too well today and there will be a lot of regrouping during the night. We shall have to wait and see where we are in the morning.'

'Perhaps Monty will be here before then.'

It was a fatuous remark, but I was only giving utterance to the one consoling thought we all had at the back of our minds. Marrable was good enough to give me the benefit of an answer in a small shrug of the shoulders and an agreed 'perhaps'.

'Oh well, I'll push off up to bed then. Good-night, sir.'

I wearily climbed the stairs to Marrable's room and sat down on the bed. After undoing my gaiters, pulling off my boots, getting rid of my tie and completing some perfunctory ablutions, I stretched out on my back under the blankets and immediately fell into a deep, dreamless sleep.

Wednesday 20 September

In no time at all I felt myself being gently shaken, while a voice I did not immediately recognize was saying, 'Wake up. Marrable here. It's two o'clock. Time for your trick.'

'Oh my God, sir, already? I don't seem to have been asleep more than five minutes.'

'You have. Don't worry. I came up to see how you were about midnight, and you were out, right out, and boy do I need that bed. Come on. There's a brew for you downstairs. Take your stuff with you. There's an officers' kit store in the cloakroom by the front door.'

Once up and moving about, I began to feel more awake and, after having had the mug of tea Marrable had left for me and having seated myself comfortably on one of the chairs in the control point, I rather enjoyed the somewhat eerie experience of waiting with the signals orderly, by a silent wireless set, in the now dimly lit and shadowy hall. The orderly, head sunk on his chest, headphones on his ears, one arm resting on the table, the other dangling by his side, was dozing again after being aroused by my arrival, while a pencil that had been between his fingers lay where it had fallen on the floor. 'Let the poor devil alone,' I thought. 'He'll brace up quick enough if anything comes over the air.'

There were two other officers on duty in the building, one on each floor to look after the patients, the rest were asleep in various rooms on the top storey which, in normal circumstances, would have been occupied by hotel staff. Now and again my head would nod and I would get up from my chair and take a short tour round the hospital. Once I lit a cigarette and, concealing it carefully in my hand, smoked it outside the service door where I had watched the Dutch nurse set off into the dark.

It was still as dark and as quiet, except perhaps that the distant rumbling away to the south seemed more insistent, or was that wishful thinking? I had not yet, even for a moment, doubted the ability of the Second Army to reach us, but I was beginning to look for its arrival like a man meeting a girl off an overdue train. Another twenty-four hours and everything would be running short: rations, ammunition, morphia, blood for transfusion, penicillin and other drugs and medicaments, bandages and dressings. By now the 4th Brigade should have been firmly established astride the northern approaches to the town, screening the vital Bridge from counter-attacks, while Horrocks' armour came pouring over in an irresistible flood to inundate the flat northern plains of Germany, and to lap at the gates of Berlin. But where exactly stood the Brigade now? Where the Battalion? Where were George Lea, Richard Lonsdale and Dan Webber? How was it I was still half way between the dropping zone and the objective – a lodger in an unfamiliar unit with which I had had no previous connection and whose people I did not know, and it was the morning of the third day? I let the cool night air refresh me a little longer, then ground out my cigarette and turned back into the hotel. It might be incomprehensible but there was nothing I could do about it.

At five o'clock, the time set for reveille, when it was still dark, the hospital started to come to life. The more severely wounded, who had been doped with morphia, returned in ones and twos from the merciful void of painless oblivion to the cruel reality of throbbing wounds and immobilized, aching limbs, stiffened by the hours on the hard stretchers. Some, who were lucky, lay on mattresses obtained from the hotel, but one and all needed to relieve nature and the shouts of 'orderly' became more and more frequent and the groans and mutterings multiplied. Soon, to this medley was added the tramp of hobnail boots, as the Royal Army Medical Corps went about its work. The electric lights blazed again and the tasks of washing and feeding got under way.

I was back in the control point and had asked the radio operator to try and raise Division for the latest news, surmising the CO would like to be briefed as soon as he appeared. The operator was still fiddling with the knobs, when a whiff of pipe tobacco and a friendly 'how goes it?' announced his arrival. I gave him my report and then, seeing how freshly shaved and immaculate he looked, hastened to the kitchen in search of hot water, collecting my towel and razor from the kit store on the way. The first person I saw on entering the kitchen was my Dutch nurse, looking as fresh and trim and unconcerned as if the war was a thousand miles away. I stood in the doorway gaping and she, on seeing me, gave a little trill of laughter, seized my hand and pulled me into the room.

'You do look funny,' she giggled, 'as if you had seen a ghost. I told you I would come back.'

I made no attempt to remove my hand from hers, but stood looking at her foolishly, aware of a strong feeling of emotion, of pleasure mixed with relief.

'When did you get back, nurse?'

'About half an hour ago.'

'But I didn't expect you so early. What made you come so soon?'

'It was safer. If there is to be any fighting it will begin at daybreak and then it will be dangerous outside.'

She spoke in a matter-of-fact voice, as if she was discussing the prospect of rain and the risks of being caught without an umbrella. She released my hand and I asked, 'How are your parents?'

'Worried, like everyone else is, but quite safe, thank you. We are living in the cellar now, and the only trouble is it gets very cold down there at night.'

'The only trouble.' I felt humbled and looked away, becoming aware for the first time of the other people in the room. The other three ladies were there again and so also was a man in civilian clothes wearing a clerical collar, who was in the act of clearing an embroidered cloth off the kitchen table. The little nurse, seeing a look of enquiry on my face, said, 'That is our priest. He has just conducted a short service for us. That is another reason why we came back early. It would not have been so easy for us to pray together later.'

I did not feel I had anything to say after that. The ladies had the fire going in the kitchen range, and were boiling kettles of water preparatory to starting their washing rounds of the wounded. I filled an enamel drinking mug with hot water, waved her a good-bye and made my way to the small room being used as an operating theatre, where I had noticed a conveniently placed mirror when being shown round the day before. This room was quite small, oblong-shaped, with a window in one of the long sides and a door at one end of the other. It contained four trestle tables, three ranged against the walls and the other set in the middle as an operating table, and a couple of chairs. On the side-tables were placed bowls of antiseptic fluids in which lay instruments, anaesthetic apparatus, dressings, vials of penicillin and catgut. On the floor were buckets.

When I started to shave it was just beginning to get light outside but, with the curtains drawn and the electric light on, I could not appreciate this; nor guess that somewhere not very far away a German officer was counting the seconds off on his watch to the hour of six o'clock, now imminent, when he would give the signal for an unheralded and furious cascade of mortar shells to fall on the area of Divisional Headquarters, whose main centre, the Hartenstein Hotel, was only four hundred yards down the road to Utrecht, and on the north east rim of which area, athwart the line of German attack and on the most tactically vital crossroads, in all its innocence reposed the Dressing Station.

At six o'clock precisely when the noise began, so entirely unexpected and thunderous, I dropped the razor and stood, momentarily, in stunned surprise, gazing at the gilt mirror dancing crazily on the wall before my face, before I hurled myself with all speed under the table. Lying there, I gradually realized that the noise was that of mortar shells with which I was now familiar. I next concluded I was in no immediate danger and presently climbed shakily to my feet, retrieved the razor, completed my shave with a hurried stroke up my left cheek, and then retreated expeditiously into the hall where a small knot of officers, gathered round the control point, was being addressed by Marrable. He beckoned me over. 'I was just saying, we must expect this sort of thing from now on until the Second Army arrives. I have not had any hard gen from Division, but the enemy is bound to regard it as a priority target and plaster it with all they've got which, incidentally as you all know, Intelligence did not think could amount to very much. The walls of this building should be proof against mortars, and they are unlikely to shell one marked as we are by large Red Crosses deliberately. Our immediate task must be to get the wounded away from the windows and to barricade them. Each officer will report back here when he considers his ward to be in a fit state of siege. Any questions? Right. Carry on.'

I lingered behind until the others had gone, not having yet been detailed to a ward, and not being sure whether I was meant to go back into reception, and enquired of Marrable what he would like me to do. He paused in the act of re-lighting his pipe, and turned to study a list of names on a plan of the building lying on the counter.

'You had better go up and help Clifford Simmons on the first floor, here,' he pointed to the plan, 'at any rate for the time being. I will try again to find out if your battalion is anywhere on the map. I take it you would still like to rejoin, if it is at all possible?'

'Yes indeed, sir.'

'Right then. I'll let you know as soon as I hear anything.'

All this time the racket was going on unabated outside. Doors and windows rattled continuously, while every now and again the building shook and trembled. In the pre-operative ward, formerly the main hotel lounge, there was a fall of soot down the chimney that rolled forward over the hearth in a dirty cloud. I did not relish the idea of going upstairs to the next floor, where there would be less in the way of solid protection from the mortar bombs, but it never occurred to me for a moment that it was a matter for debate, like so many of my actions of the previous day had been. This was an order. I would, without question, have gone and sat on the roof itself if told to.

As it was, the situation on the first floor was hair-raising enough. Many of the mortar bombs were exploding on hitting the trees, which abounded in the grounds of the hotel, and were spraying jagged lumps of metal about, splintering windows and causing many of the wounded to lie apprehensively on their stretchers or mattresses with their blankets drawn over their heads. Captain Simmons was crawling from man to man on his hands and knees, and it was in this posture, also, that I crossed the room from the door and sidled up to him. I noted that all the windows had already been shattered and the din was appalling, since sound waves from outside could now dash themselves unimpeded against the eardrums. The hotel had become like a small island in the midst of a tropical storm, and to all those within, wounded, doctors, nurses, padres, orderlies, the battle was experienced as a frightful hurricane of noise. On the ever prevailing wind of mortar bomb explosions was borne, at length, the intermittent but thunderous tempest of tank and artillery shells, the scattered vicious hail from small-arms and automatics, the screech of roof-hopping fighter planes, the crash of ack-ack, and lulls of soft moanings, sinister calms, as in the eye of a storm, which every ear strained anxiously to interpret. While into the harbour of this island was spewed the wreckage, human jetsam cast up helplessly by the tide of war, the doctors picking over it like beachcombers to salvage what might conceivably be used again in the currency of life. Even an intact window had a barrier effect, placing what was happening outside at a distance from what was happening within, but once shattered the two worlds commingled, and the room became a mere recess in the open arena of battle.

It was a nightmare, and in the grotesqueness of nightmares it was possible, by stepping out of the room onto the landing and closing the door, to find instant relative calm and normality. For the doctors and others, to whom this avenue of escape was always, theoretically, open, the duty of remaining within the room to care for the wounded, often entailing exposure of their persons in silhouette against gaping windows, was a severe and exhausting discipline. For the wounded, some of whom actually received fresh wounds from shell splinters or flying glass as they lay helpless on the floor, it was sheer, unrelieved hell.

I touched Simmons on the shoulder, announcing myself by name and unit. 'I've been sent up to give you a hand. I got tacked onto your outfit yesterday, if you remember.'

Simmons gave me a quick smile. 'Let's cut out the formality old man, call me Clifford. This is one hell of a situation. We need a mattress to block the lower part of this window with, and it means tipping one of these poor devils out onto the floor until we can get hold of a stretcher or something to put him on.'

He spoke loudly, almost shouting to make himself heard above the din, and before either of us could utter another word there was a hoarse response from one of the recumbent figures on the floor. 'You can have mine, sir.'

The voice came from a Sergeant, his right leg wrapped in a blood-stained bandage, the trouser split up to the knee, who seeing Simmons about to remonstrate continued urgently, 'I've made myself comfortable in worse places than this and it won't be for long.'

There was a pause, and then Simmons made a brisk acceptance of the offer. 'That's very good of you, Sergeant, very good indeed, thank you.'

We extracted the mattress from under the Sergeant, half lifting, half rolling him, while he bared his teeth in a mirthless grin of pain that gradually relaxed as he subsided back onto the wooden floor. Then carrying it before us, shieldlike, we used it to block the lower part of the window.

'That's better,' said Simmons, straightening up and dusting off his hands. 'Now, let's look at these wounds, some of them will need cleaning up and re-dressing. The CO was planning to allot me a time in the theatre this morning to see to the ones that got left over from yesterday. Can you give pentothal?'

'Yes, I've given a few. But why me? What about the surgical teams. They've got proper anaesthetists.'

'Oh they're working in nearby buildings we're using as surgical annexes. There isn't room for them here. The drill has been to unload onto them all the cases, like abdomens, heads and major amps, we think we can't do ourselves.'

'After they've had shock treatment.'

'That's it.'

'I get you. But how, may I ask, do you unload them in this?' I jerked my head towards the window.

'Wait for a lull, I suppose,' said Simmons, shrugging his shoulders.

'We had planned to be here only until yesterday, and up to now it has worked beautifully. Anyway, let's get cracking. You check up the ones on that side of the room. Try to sort them out into an order of priority. Only those requiring an anaesthetic for an otherwise too painful cleaning up of their wounds are for our theatre. Any other treatments will have to be given in here.'

We crawled from man to man, glancing at the field labels attached to some part of the clothing, undoing dressing and examining wounds which, now being in most cases more than twenty-four hours old, were beginning to suppurate and stink. The men endured the examinations for the most part silently, or with a mere inspiratory hiss to betray their suffering, and all the time the noise outside continued unabated, making us flinch involuntarily whenever it came close. The protection afforded by the mattress helped, although its protection may have been more psychological than actual, insecurely lodged as it was on the window-sill. Also, with the passing of time we gradually became inured to the monotonous explosions. We had the distraction of our work and had been joined by a Corporal to assist with the note-taking which speeded things up. After about an hour of it Simmons and I had completed our survey. The wounded who needed theatre treatment had been identified and listed in order of priority, and other treatments written up. Leaving the Corporal in charge to carry out instructions, we went downstairs to report to the control point.

'May we use the theatre now, sir?' Simmons asked the CO. 'There are one or two chaps we ought to get on with as soon as possible. I though Mawson could give the anaesthetics.'

Marrable quizzed me about my experience in this field. I told him I had regularly given anaesthetics as casualty officer and later house surgeon at my London hospital, even major ones on occasions.

'Right ho,' he said at length. 'Go ahead. By the way, I've not been able to get any news of the 11th. Division thinks your CO may be in the bag and wants me to take you on my strength for the rest of the operation.'

I was thankful and not altogether surprised at this news. It was quite obvious that things were not going at all as hoped and expected, and it was now tacitly accepted we had suffered a very sharp reverse and that the timely arrival of the Second Army was the one remaining peg upon which a successful outcome to the battle hung. I certainly did not relish the idea of being cast adrift from my present anchorage to search for my own unit in the middle of this bombardment. Having had the responsibility of taking battle decisions removed from my shoulders and having found myself, so far, able to cope with the duties I had been given, I was very content to stay put. Besides there was the Dutch nurse. I had thought of her as I had been working upstairs, wondering where she was and what she was doing. It was impossible to feel anything disastrous could happen while she and the other ladies were with us in a building plastered with Red Crosses. What better place was there to be in at this juncture. What luck I had had so far. What astounding good luck.

'I'll need bearers to bring the cases down,' said Simmons. 'The Corporal up there has the tally and knows what order to send them in.'

'I'll take care of it.'

As we opened the door to the theatre, the sound of explosions met us with a new fury. I stood aghast at the sight of the room. For although it had already been used that morning by another pair of doctors who had done their best to leave it tidy, it bore no resemblance to the one I had had my shave in some hours before. In place of ordered cleanliness was something approaching chaos. The windows, which had been curtained and intact, were now gaping holes bordered by wicked glass stilettos, while the once good curtains themselves were shot and torn and ragged. The floor was covered by a layer of plaster fallen from the ceiling, mixed with blood, spilled water and antiseptic, and pieces of khaki clothing cut from the wounded. Dust was everywhere and the noise appalling. I expostulated, 'How in the hell can we work in here?'

'Don't know, old man, but there's nowhere else.' Simmons smiled briefly. 'Come on. I'll start on the primus and try to get some water boiling.'

I flicked down the electric light switch, thinking it would be better to keep what was left of the curtains drawn across the window, but it was dead. I glanced at the bulb, blackened and burnt out.

'I'd better try and scrounge a bulb from somewhere. This one's had it.'

I addressed my remark to the kneeling Simmons, who replied without leaving off his efforts to pump life into the stove, 'Oh, I shouldn't bother. It's likely the main has gone, and if it hasn't it won't survive this lot. I'm more worried about the water supply and drains. We'll have to make do with daylight.'

Daylight! Apprehensively I advanced on the window and tore the tattered curtains aside in a rapid movement. Framed through the jagged glass was a shrubbery backed by a thick cluster of trees, through which the gables of a house were just discernible. The atmosphere was thick with smoke, and the woods had a derelict appearance, the branches of the trees hanging in festoons like peeling wallpaper. My mind was functioning very slowly. It seemed such a hopeless situation to try to grapple with. How could one concentrate on giving intravenous injections with this horror at one's very elbow. Almost unconscious of what I was doing I seized a chair, and began savagely to clear the window frame of broken glass; better outside than in. I ducked as an ominous whistle volleyed through the trees, and then forced myself to walk measuredly over to the table, where the vials of pentothal were laid, ready to be mixed with those containing sterile distilled water, and where the syringes and needles were lying in a shallow, lidded tray of methylated spirit. After sterilizing my hands in a bowl of lysol, made by dissolving the appropriate tablets in water, I took one of the syringes out and assembled it. Then I turned and faced into the room, the window on my left, the door in the far corner of the wall on my right, and Simmons at the other end of the operating table. He now had one eye closed and his tongue was protruding surreptitiously through a corner of his mouth, while he concentrated on threading catgut through curved needles.

'Clifford, I'm ready, are you? Because if so, I'll go and hurry up the bearers.'

'Quite ready, old man. Bring 'em in. Sooner we start the better.'

Simmons again spoke without taking his eyes off what he was doing. When I came to think about it, he was one of those people who was always doing something. He was spare, dark and restless. If he sat or stood it was never with legs crossed or arms folded, but always with some work he was doing with his hands, rolling cigarettes, scouring out the bowl of his pipe, mending splints, writing in a notebook, counting pills or improvising a new surgical gadget, which seemed utterly to absorb him. I envied him this trait, for he seemed to have an imperviousness to the immediate danger of spraying mortar bomb fragments that was quite exceptional even in this community of, to me, exceptional men.

I was about to move over to open the door when there was a noise outside, and the stretcher bearers entered carrying in the first patient and deposited him on the table. His eyes were closed, his lips dry and bloodless, and he breathed heavily through his open mouth, across the rim of which he endlessly passed his tongue, like a metronome in slow motion.

'Right, old man,' Simmons was undoing the bandage on the man's leg, 'put him to sleep.'

I bent over and said into the man's ear, 'Look, old chap, I'm going to put you to sleep now. It'll only be a prick in the arm.'

The tongue stopped its rhythmical movements, the mouth closed and opened once, twice and a third time, and then gave utterance to a scarcely audible whisper, 'OK, sir, save my leg, won't you.'

'Yes, of course. Don't you worry.'

I rolled up the man's sleeve, straightened his arm and swabbed the soft skin in the fold of the elbow with methylated spirit.

'Clench your fist hard, old chap. That's right.'

The veins did not stand out well at first as the loss of blood had impoverished the circulation. I made an abortive attempt to insert the needle, and then asked Simmons to twist the sleeve tight round the arm above the elbow so as to dam back the venous stream. The arm started to tremble and I made another attempt, sliding the needle through the skin and probing for a vein, as a blind man feels for a keyhole. Beyond the window the mortar shells scythed and crashed through the trees, detonating like depth charges in the green-brown sea of the undergrowth. Anxious and sweating, I repeatedly advanced the needle and withdrew the plunger of the syringe until, at last, with relief, I saw a dark purple spurt of blood discolour the anaesthetic. I nodded to Simmons to loosen the sleeve and then slowly injected the pentothal, watching the man's face all the time for the lolling of the head and in-sucking of the cheeks denoting the first deep breaths of unconsciousness.

'OK, Clifford. Go to work. He's out.'

Simmons dealt with the wound swiftly and methodically, cutting out all hopelessly damaged tissue with a sharp scalpel until the blood flowed again brightly. Most of the belly of the calf muscle had to be sacrificed, but the bones were intact and the blood supply to the foot seemed sufficient to maintain its viability. At the end of the operation there was simply a large wedge-shaped gash that would be expected to become infected, but being laid widely open would drain any putrid matter through the flavine-soaked gauze with which it was packed, gradually shrink, and heal up from the bottom. We dealt with a succession of wounds in this way, ducking and flinching involuntarily with each of the louder, nearer explosions that loosened more plaster flakes off the ceiling and shredded more of the branches outside.

After the first anaesthetic I gained a new feeling of confidence in my ability, not just to put a man to sleep and wake him up again, but to take whatever might come my way. As the passage of time failed to add more to what I had already been able to endure, it accelerated the seasoning process that hardens control. The consoling thought came to me, as I brooded at the head of the table with my finger on the pulse of an unconscious patient, that, as I might very well be killed at any one of these passing moments, it implied I was, in fact, facing death all the time and that, after all, it was not such a very difficult thing to do when one got used to it. Being under orders I knew I must do my duty regardless of what I felt, and that knowledge also had a steadying effect. Even so, between cases, Simmons and I were glad to lie on the floor under the tables, as the battle appeared to be steadily increasing in ferocity. Bren guns and Spandaus snarled at each other like hungry carnivores, echoed by the lesser killers, rifles, Stens and other repeaters, stalking each other through the disintegrating jungle of trees and houses. Once a piece of metal whirred through the window and embedded itself in the wall opposite, and a rifle went off so close outside I thought it had been fired by somebody in the room. Then the mortaring stopped as suddenly as it had begun, and all the world was filled with a rattling and banging, as though we were in an ironmonger's shop in an earthquake.

At the height of this commotion, while Simmons and I were lying under tables, another case was brought in and a voice, which we recognized as the CO's and brought us scrambling to our feet, shouted, 'Clifford, where in the blazes are you? Oh there you are! You've got to do something quick. We've got Padre Benson here and he's in a very bad way.'

Simmons, who was looking rather sheepish, drew his mouth into a hard line when he saw the padre, whose face and clothes were covered with a mask of blood and plaster, and whose right arm was dangling grotesquely over the side of the stretcher.

'What happened, sir?'

'He was brought down like this from one of the rooms upstairs. We've had four hits by eighty-eight millimetre guns on two of the small wards. The top storey's an absolute shambles, half the roof's down. Can't stop. Good luck boys.'

Simmons took one look at the arm. 'That'll have to come off for a start. Get him under.' I wiped the blood and plaster off the Padre's gashed face and pulled the lids of one eye apart.

'No need. He's out cold already.'

The proper amputation saws were with the surgical teams in the other buildings but it was found that an escape file might be used as a substitute. These files, issued with the escape kits and presumably intended for prison bars, had a perforation at one end. By attaching a piece of wire to this perforation and clipping a pair of artery forceps to the other end, one could make a two-handed job of it.

Oblivious of the din, even oblivious of the shouts that had been added to the bedlam, Clifford worked at getting the Padre's arm off and I worked at sewing up his face. Simmons had his back to the door and therefore paid no attention to it when it was suddenly, noisily, flung open, but I saw it out of the corner of my eye and glanced up, thinking it would be orderlies with yet another case. Slowly, unbelievingly, I straightened up and raised my arms above my head, tissue forceps still in my left hand, needle holder in my right, since I was staring wide-eyed at an automatic sub-machine gun levelled straight at my chest. I stood rooted in this attitude, my eyes travelling slowly down the spotted camouflage smock to grey trousers tucked into jack boots and back again, taking in the hand grenades dangling from the belt, and past the gun, the hard peremptory line of the mouth, the begrimed face and bloodshot, tired-looking, but very alert eyes beneath the coal-skuttle helmet. I felt I was part of a still from a movie arrested at a frame that would never move on. Then I heard myself saying in a small flat voice, 'Better get your hands up, Clifford. There's a German behind you.'

Simmons paid no attention for a second or two and then, as my words sunk in, he looked up and raised his eyebrows to start a question which died on his lips as he saw the expression on my face, and he raised his hands without saying a word and turned cautiously round towards the door. Having found I was able to speak, I cleared my throat nervously and, holding the German's eye, said, pointing first to Simmons and then myself, 'Doctor. Doctor.'

Then I added, pointing to the unconscious figure on the table and indicating the dog-collar, 'Pastor. Pastor.'

The German took a menacing step into the room, jerking the barrel of his gun upwards as he did so, unmistakably indicating that he wished our hands to point only to the ceiling. Then, behind him in the doorway I saw my little Dutch nurse and I felt sick and wondered if I was going to faint, as I did once when a student watching my first major operation. They had called it a vaso-vagal attack and advised me, if I felt like it again, to take a deep breath and pull in my stomach, which I now did, several times. She stepped into the room and started to speak rapidly in German, until the German interrupted her with a stream of shouted words directed at Simmons and myself, off whom he never took his eyes for a moment. When he stopped the nurse said quietly, 'He is asking if you have any arms concealed in here.'

'Tell him, no, of course not,' Simmons said. 'Do we look as if we had? Tell him the Minister of God here needs our help badly and we must get on with our work.'

The nurse and the German spoke together for a few minutes again and I could feel the tension relaxing. Eventually she smiled at us and said the German accepted our word that we were unarmed, and we could continue our work, but we must realize we were now prisoners of the victorious German army and would be allowed to do only what it permitted. The German took another few steps into the room and, reaching up, pulled Simmons hands down from above his head and pointed to the body on the stretcher. He did the same to me and then returned to the door, from where he stood watching as we silently began again to mend the padre. I looked surreptitiously at the nurse, who was leaning against the wall just inside the room. 'God, that girl's got nerve,' I thought, 'nerve and a lot more beside.' I was feeling the reaction. My hands shook uncontrollably as I inserted the last few stitches in the padre's face. My legs felt weak, and I would have liked to have been able to sit down and smoke a cigarette. I looked again at the nurse.

'Can you come and help me with this bandage? I need somebody to hold his head up.'

She came over without speaking, and together we bound up the man of God, she supporting him while I placed the turns of the bandage. Simmons, having finished sewing up the stump of the padre's arm, had the nurse then help him with his bandage. He whispered to her in a conspiratorial but clearly audible fashion, 'We've got to get him to the resuscitation ward, he'll need a transfusion after losing all this blood, and with the concussion he'll need constant watching.' He looked searchingly at the nurse. 'Can you make that thick-headed German understand that?'

'Oh yes, I think so,' she said. 'He was very anxious to be correct. He was scared you were armed. Think what it must be like for him surrounded by you British in here. He will shoot from nervousness if he thinks he is threatened.'

'Surrounded by us! Threatened by us! That's a good one.' Simmons grinned. 'Do you mean to say he took the place single-handed?'

The girl smiled back. 'Oh no. A lot of them broke in through the back door, and were into the hall and all over the place before we realized what was happening. Then most of them went straight through and out the other end through reception.'

Simmons snorted. 'Using the cover of the Red Cross to gain advantage for their attacks. The blighters. We seem to be in a tough sort of spot. But never mind. Will you ask him if we can carry the padre to resuscitation?'

She nodded and walked over to the door, while Simmons and I placed ourselves in readiness to lift the stretcher off the table. The German made no objection, although he watched warily as we manoeuvred our burden out of the room. Marrable was at the control point in the hall and, seeing us as we passed through, took his pipe out of his mouth and said encouragingly, 'Good show chaps. Don't take any notice of the Jerries. Carry on as if nothing has happened.'

It was impossible, however, not to take notice of the Germans. They had a strong presence, based on the utter incongruity of their heavily armed and booted persons in the pacific precincts of the hospital. They caught the eye as a uniformed policeman might at a vicarage tea party. While they struck no great fear into their helpless captives because they gave no indication of intending wholesale murder, they nevertheless engendered an atmosphere of anxiety and depressing disappointment. The Royal Army Medical Corps of non-combatants and their suffering patients were in no position to influence events in their favour at this juncture. The discipline they had to learn was submission to the enemy. The padres, by their habitual submission to a will other than their own, were perhaps less disenfranchised and less impoverished by these circumstances than the doctors, who were now running out of vital medical supplies and losing the facilities for normal cleanliness and hygiene, without any immediate prospect of remedy. The wounded, who such a short time ago had been in the prime of their manly strength, well-armed and confident of victory, now lay helpless on blood-soaked pallets unable to move a finger to help themselves – mere bobbing corks on the current of events. They were the real losers of liberty and victims of this bitter reversal of fortune. That they never at any time, by so much as a whisper, complained of their lot must be considered an example of fortitude in the highest tradition of the British army.

We handed Padre Benson over to the blood transfusion officer and his team, whose room was three or four times bigger than the operating theatre but, with now glassless windows giving out onto the same shrubbery and woods, was in a similar state of broken disorder, and then returned to the control point, anxious to see if the CO could put us more clearly in the picture.

With the arrival of the Germans in the building there had been an unmistakable decrease in the firing, and it was not long before it died away altogether in the immediate vicinity. The CO was out of touch with Divisional Headquarters and unable to throw any further light on the situation, but it did not require much intelligent guessing to realize that it was serious.

Yet, after the neighbourhood grew quiet and the battle failed to be rejoined, someone started the acceptable rumour that the Germans must have abandoned their offensive and be withdrawing because of the arrival of the Second Army; and, since it was what we all wanted to happen, this rumour gained credence, and there was an amazing reversal of mood that afternoon that must have been extremely puzzling to the German Sergeant and his section who at that time were posted in the building. In the space, perhaps, of a couple of hours the grim, anxious, fatigue-lined faces had all turned to smiles, and the silent had become chatty and communicative. Someone struck a chord on the piano and those near burst out into a lusty rendering of 'Roll out the Barrel'. Whereas the future, a short time before, had been faced with a kind of resigned fatalism, all now cheerfully started to clear up the mess. Blankets dusty with plaster were shaken out, floors swept clean, shutters of rooms lucky enough to have them and doors giving out onto the street were flung open, so that fresh air could circulate, Medical Corps men and the ladies cleaned up the patients, and everything began to return to a semblance of normality. Simmons and I did what we could with the operating theatre, and improvised a barricade for the lower part of the window. It was hard to believe how suddenly the mental atmosphere could change but it happened again and again. Whenever the noise stopped the depression lifted. There would be a compensatory reaction of extravagant hilarity, and then, soon after, everyone would shake down to a more normal level.

I saw little or nothing of Dwyer and Adams that day. They had come under the jurisdiction of the Regimental Sergeant Major, Mr Bryson, an indispensable linchpin of the organization, and had been allotted tasks in different parts of the building.

The continued lull in the fighting enabled great strides to be made in the restoration of order in the hospital and, by late afternoon, something approaching the trim cleanliness which so impressed me when I first saw it once again prevailed. The CO, accompanied by Major Frazer, made a tour of inspection of the whole building, while we officers waited in the areas allotted to us, Simmons and I again upstairs, and personally conducted him round to each patient for whom we were responsible. The Germans hovered about in the background, suspiciously roaming through the rooms, one of them never letting Marrable out of his sight, until, just before nightfall, they all quite inexplicably left the building except for one lonely Corporal who was left as sole guard of the whole outfit. This Corporal established himself on a chair in the hall with a tommy-gun across his knees, with his eyes darting anxiously from side to side as if he were watching a tennis match.

There were by now some three hundred wounded in our building, and perhaps another two hundred spread round in the adjacent buildings commandeered for the purpose. There were also several wounded Germans, whom the RAMC had been at pains to treat with the same consideration as our own men. Evidently they had testified as much to their own officer, who had made straight for them and questioned them when he had taken the building. Doubtless, if he had not been satisfied on this point we should not have enjoyed the relative leniency afforded us during their occupation.

Before darkness fell I went to look for my Dutch nurse, determined to dissuade her from making any attempt to go home again. I found her on her knees beside a stretcher, feeding a man with bandaged eyes from a mess-tin of stew concocted for the evening meal from dehydrated meat cubes. I stood watching her silently until, having administered the last mouthful and wiped the man's lips, she clambered onto her feet and backed straight into me.

'Sorry –' she began, turning round to see who it was, then, 'Oh, I did not mean to knock into you.'

'My fault,' I said, and then added solicitously, putting a hand out to help her regain her balance, 'You look tired. Don't you think you've done enough for us today?'

'I can never do enough,' she replied simply, gently pushing past me toward a cauldron, that had been deposited at the end of the room, in order to replenish her mess tin.

I followed her over to the cauldron and silently helped her ladle stew into the tin. I found myself asking myself why it really was, I was so concerned that she should stay. She was exerting a pull on me and a wish for her company, and I think it was because, in her presence, I felt more emancipated from the grim circumstances surrounding my position in her country. It came to me as I watched her that at another time and in another place I might well have wanted to pursue her in a conventional manner, to have asked her out to a restaurant and theatre, to dances and parties, but one could hardly entertain serious romantic thoughts in a room full of wounded soldiers and the smell of sepsis and stale sweat, and with an armed German holding a watching brief. Presently I voiced the thought that had been in my mind when I first looked for her, striving to make myself sound casual and not too concerned. 'I hope you will not be thinking of going home again tonight, not now the Germans are all around and in the place.'

'I had not thought about it yet,' she replied, straightening her back and pressing a fist wearily into a spot between her hip and ribs. 'I do not think they would molest me.'

She spoke with a question in her voice and I seized upon it quickly. 'Maybe not, but they might stop you coming back.'

I searched her face, trying to anticipate her reply.

'Yes,' she said slowly, 'I think you are right, they probably would. It makes them very angry to find us helping you. If it was not for the Red Cross Convention, they would treat us very severely.'

'Then you must not think of leaving our protection until the battle is won.'

She paused, and considered for a moment. 'But what about my parents? They will worry.'

'It might be worse for them if the Germans followed you home.' I was talking at random about something I knew nothing at all about, but I went on, 'They could punish you all then if they had a mind to.

Perhaps it will be possible to get a message through to them?'

'Do you think so?'

'I don't know but we can find out.'

We went into the kitchen, where some of the Dutch ladies might be found at this time of the day, and I stood to one side while she and they engaged in a long conference. It was aggravating not being able to understand what was being said, as I would have dearly liked to be able to put my oar in. My relief was considerable when she turned to include me in the conversation, and said gravely in English, 'We all think it would be better to stay here under the circumstances. I will send a message if I can. Perhaps the priest will be able to deliver it. They have not stopped him moving freely among our people so far.'

'I'm very glad, and feel sure it cannot be for long. The liberation army must be very near now.'

I said good-night, and made my way to the control point to see if there was anything more for me to do. Simmons met me as I entered the hall.

'I've been looking for you old man. No guard duties for us tonight. We've been tossing up for billets and guess what. You and I have won the cupboard under the stairs.'

'Whizzo,' I said.

The rooms upstairs occupied by the officers the previous night had been rendered untenable by the day's bombardment, and the cupboard under the stairs was the safest place in the building except the cellar, and nice and quiet. Simmons explained there would be no formal watch-keeping as some officers would be sleeping in the control point, and others would be dotted about downstairs, some in the passage leading to the service door and others near other exits. The wounded, many of whom would sleep only fitfully, and the NCOs in the wards with them also had ears subconsciously on the *qui vive*. We did not know exactly what to expect but many would be instantly awake in the event of any kind of rumpus or anything unusual.

'Come on,' said Simmons. 'If tomorrow's going to be another day like this we shall need all the sleep we can get.'

'I'm with you.'

We collected our gear from the cache in the cloakroom by the main entrance and made for the cupboard. Simmons flung open the door with the air of a conjuror producing a rabbit out of a hat.

'There! What do you think of that?'

'Just the job. But the floor looks a bit hard.' I was thinking of the comfort of Marrable's bed the night before.

'You'll get used to it. Here, I'll go in and you pass me the blankets. It'll be best to put them on the floor and then try to roll them over us.'

Simmons doubled himself up and disappeared into the dark hole. I fed him the blankets one by one and he arranged them on the floor. Then I went in and we sat down side by side together, took off our boots and loosened our ties. Then, using haversacks as pillows, we lay on our sides back to back and I pulled the cupboard door closed, so that the only light came as a faint glimmer through the key-hole. I gazed at it for a little while. My thoughts, as they became liberated from the constraints of time, began to jump inconsequentially from image to image, but never far from the figure of a fair, slim girl with gentle eyes.

'This is all right, Clifford. I think I'll go to sleep now.'

Thursday 21 September

At 4 a.m. a corporal of the RAMC tugged agitatedly at the door of the cupboard under the stairs and, having opened it, shone a torch on the recumbent figures on the floor inside. He hesitated for a split second before making any fresh move and then vigorously shook the arm of the nearer sleeper.

'Wake up, sir. Wake up.'

I stirred, opened my eyes unwillingly and then became fully awake in an instant as it dawned on me where I was.

'What is it?' I asked in a forced whisper. It was still dark. The crouching man behind the torch was an indistinct shadow. Simmons slept on.

'We've been liberated, sir.'

'Liberated?'

'During the night.'

I sat up abruptly. 'Do you mean the Second Army – ?'

'No, sir,' the voice behind the torch sounded apologetic, 'I'm afraid not. But,' here it waxed enthusiastic again, 'our lads have returned and we're back in our own lines.'

I did not know quite what to make of this having heard nothing in the night, and pushed my knee hard into Simmons' rump. 'Did you hear all that?'

He groaned and stirred, and then sat up.

'We've been freed.'

'Yes, I heard, but it seems all the more a good reason for staying here in bed.'

At this the torch waved about in an agitated fashion and the voice said, 'CO's calling an officers' conference. He would like you to report to him at once in the kitchen. OK, sir?'

'OK. Thanks. Come on, Clifford. Up we get. My God, it's chilly.'

'How the hell do you suppose they did it?' Simmons said, half to himself, as he struggled to put on his boots. 'I didn't hear a thing in the night, did you?'

'Not a thing. But hurry up, we'll soon know.'

We scrambled out into the dim void of the hall, which was illuminated by a single candle, stuck in a delicately executed candlestick of Delft china standing on the counter of the control point. After the fuggy atmosphere of the cupboard the air of the hall seemed fresh, except for the fact that it was tainted with the strong odour of excreta and suppuration, which had become as inseparable from our daily existence as fatigue and noise.

In the kitchen Marrable was sitting on a table, his feet on a chair, elbows on knees and hands clasped round the bowl of his pipe, on which he drew silently as he contemplated the officers gathering from various parts of the building. We grouped ourselves round the kitchen range, warming ourselves by the fire kept going all the night, and there was a hum of expectant conversation as we speculated on this latest, apparently favourable turn of events.

'Right, chaps,' Marrable took the pipe from his mouth and knocked it out against his boot, 'this is the form. Div HQ at the Hartenstein is now the nerve centre of a new concentration of all Airborne forces remaining under the General's command. All available troops have been withdrawn into the Oosterbeek area and we are holding a bridgehead based on a chain ferry still usable over the river. We have to see it remains in our hands as it is the only certain river crossing available to the Second Army, who are through Nijmegen.'

'We've lost the Arnhem Bridge then,' an officer commented.

'So it is understood, and Jerry is plastering the road south with eighty-eights and making the going very tough for our tanks. During the night our chaps here have been trying to widen the circumference of the bridgehead perimeter, and have succeeded in infiltrating through here. The Jerries pulled out and we are now just inside our own lines. The General reckons we can hold the perimeter with what we've got for another day or two, but the Germans are bound to do their damnest to push us out and we're very vulnerable on the edge on this main road. We are expecting supply drops every day from now on, and the Polish Brigade is being put down on the other side of the river to secure the south bank for the ferry. At the best the Second Army will come over the river tonight and our troubles will be over, at the worst we may have to wait another night or two, but with the supply drops we should manage to hold on. I am bringing one of the surgical teams back into the Schoonoord as things are now too difficult for them where they are. The same arrangements will be in force today as yesterday. Major cases will be operated on by the surgical team who will, therefore, have priority on the theatre. I shall have to fit you others in as best I can, depending on the fresh casualties we receive today. Any of you who happen not to be engaged in your wards at any time must report to me – there will be plenty of jobs going. There's little more than half an hour left to daylight now, and I want everyone shaved with something in his stomach before dawn. So get cracking. Any questions?'

There was a general dispersal and I approached Marrable with my now stock question. 'May I ask, sir, if the 11th has been heard of yet?'

'Ah, yes,' Marrable paused in the act of re-lighting his pipe, 'I was going to tell you. Major Lonsdale has collected elements of your battalion, and of other units, and brought them under his command in what is now to be known as Lonsdale Force. He is holding the south-east corner of the perimeter with his HQ in the church.'

I well remembered the spot from yesterday morning.

'That is indeed good news, sir. Should I not now rejoin him?'

'I understand your concern,' said Marrable in a sympathetic tone of voice, 'but there is already an RAP there under Captain Martin. All units are mixed up now and I want you to remain on my strength until the whole show is over.'

That the battle now made some kind of sense, and a definite way still lay open to the south across the river had a most encouraging and steadying effect on everyone. Even if we had not lost faith we had been sorely tried and, although the main objective had not been achieved, it was good for our morale to know the best had apparently been made of a bad job, and that the day could yet be saved if only the perimeter and ferry crossing were held for long enough. Although a non-combatant I had now become identified absolutely with the fighting men, and even thought of myself in terms of being one of them; as a boxer who, entering the ring more intent on avoiding than giving hurt, arrives at a moment of realization that his opponent is swayed by no such consideration, rather on doing as much damage as he possibly can, and has to be properly taken on and stopped. Whereas during the first two days I had never been able to believe in the possibility of disaster overtaking our enterprise, and had been unprepared and almost indignant when danger threatened me personally, it now dawned on me quite plainly that the issue was now, for the remnant of which I was a part, no survival against a chance of survival. Either we would win or the Germans would win, and if they won there might not be too many of us left to tell the tale.

It was difficult to know quite what to expect from the Germans in the way of attack, for the situation was manifestly different from what it had been yesterday. In the jargon of war communiques it had ceased to be fluid and was now stabilized, not as had been hoped with the enemy on the defensive but, at least, to a point where the boundaries of no man's land were clearly discernible and known to both sides. It might be supposed that the technique used by the enemy to deal with a division at large would be different to that needed to give a *coup de grâce* to a confined remnant at bay, but, in fact, one of the most surprising things, at least to those seeing it through in the Dressing Station, was the sameness of it all.

A doctor in every action is always relatively protected from the naked atmosphere of aggression that envelops visible antagonists. His is essentially a war of sounds. He seldom sees the enemy in action, only hears their efforts at destruction and he learns, perhaps as quickly as a combatant soldier, to interpret the language of lethal noises, to distinguish idle chatter from dangerous talk, to know when to disregard and when to pay heed. The rifleman who must sight to kill looks out on a changing world of moving targets. The doctor's vision is focused downwards on immobile, sanguinous objects lying beneath his hands while only his ears range over the battlefield. He may be more comfortable in body but hardly more so in spirit. He can do little or nothing to influence events, cannot resort to violent action to relieve his feelings and must submit utterly to the discipline of his profession, allowing himself to serve as a one-way channel through which succour and healing may be brought to the wounded, without counting the cost to himself or considering his own position. If the enemy choose to kill him, he must submit to that, even if it should be unintentional. If his own side abandons the field to fight another day, he must submit to the needs of the wounded and be abandoned with them. Let it not be wondered at, if the fabric sometimes cracks, rather that in the main it holds tolerably together.

At precisely six o'clock, as on the previous morning, the Germans opened fire on the area with mortars and shortly added to the weight of the bombardment with shells from self-propelled 88mm guns.

The same sickening feeling of apprehension settled in the pit of my, and I supposed, every stomach, and the same macabre scenes developed as already wounded men received fresh injuries as they lay helpless; jagged pieces of metal whirred indiscriminately through broken windows whenever a missile was exploded at high level by a tree, or when a near miss landed in the road or garden immediately outside. The noise quickly built up to a racket exceeding anything we had yet had to experience. It became clear the Germans meant serious business, intending to crush as quickly as they could the opposition of what they now must think was a ragged and insignificant force. They must have already taken a sufficient number of prisoners, dead or alive, to give them legitimate grounds for supposing the remnant facing them was negligible, at least in terms of the numbers they themselves now seemed able to deploy. Nor could they afford to exert less than their maximum effort to gain control of the ferry, as vital to them as it was for us, for on it depended the safety of their homeland, and its loss could be an immediate prelude to their complete defeat. To us, for the same reason, it was an equally vital possession, as the only avenue of not only relief but withdrawal, and without which the depleted Airborne Division possibly faced complete annihilation. The battle for it was, therefore, quite simply to the death. It was fought with an unrelenting ferocity on both sides without thought of quarter: fought by the Germans in an urgent frenzy of determination to consolidate the partial victory they had already gained, yet with a growing sense of respect for their opponents, the British, who despite their disparity in fire-power and numbers, were as stubborn and tenacious as their breed can be and held on and on, fighting back with an illogical sense of superiority that would not countenance the possibility of defeat.

The suddenness of the barrage startled the hospital into accelerated life, rather in the same way as a lifted flagstone sends ants and other small creatures a-scurrying. All grades of staff appeared from their nocturnal corners as if by magic, and in a matter of minutes the wards and passages were thronged. In the kitchen I shared a mess-tin, quarter full of hot water for shaving, with Simmons and, pausing now and again to sip from a mug of the concoction of hot tea that passed as breakfast, grimly contemplated the prospect of another morning in the ward if it was to be worse than the last. When the Dutch ladies, including my nurse, came into the kitchen from the cellar where they had spent the night, to collect water to start washing rounds of the wounded, I had my battle-dress blouse off and was in my shirt sleeves, a towel round my neck and shoulders and lather on my face. She looked crumpled and dishevelled after her fully clothed night's sleep. We could hardly have seemed less alluring to each other, but the greeting and glances we exchanged were warm, and seemed to spin more gossamer to enlarge the web of mutual interest I, at least, felt was entangling us.

'They always start this in the middle of my shave.' I felt a need to explain my appearance.

'You should get up earlier,' she bantered. 'I have heard in England you are accustomed to stay in bed much later than we are over here –' we both froze as a shell exploded in the shrubbery outside. The kitchen had the same garden aspect as the theatre but the windows were smaller and set higher in the wall, and it felt immeasurably safer. I glowered in the direction of the window.

'I expect we go to bed later. You must come and find out when this,' I nodded at the window, 'when this is all over.'

'I should like that.' She threw me a little smile and with a slight inclination of her head moved away and joined the other ladies.

I watched her for a minute or two, thoughtfully wiping the remnant of shaving soap off my face, then put my blouse on and went in the direction of the control point, in order to confirm my allocation to the ward and stow my washing gear in the officers' cache.

On the crossroads outside the hotel a pair of our anti-tank guns and their crews were dug into deep pits. The Germans, intent on their destruction, sent mortar bombs into the area like shoals of fish going over a waterfall, rattling the building with a constant shimmering vibration and causing dust to exhale from every crevice, and plaster to flake down from the ceilings like snow onto the hapless patients beneath.

In the ward upstairs, where Simmons and I were again working together, the greater desperation of the wounded could be gauged from the fact that compared with yesterday when they had lain for the most part quietly and contemplatively, they were now finding it necessary to bolster up their spirits and distract their minds from their intolerable predicament in various ways, according to individual temperament. Some made loud facetious remarks, at which they themselves would laugh immoderately. Others would let loose the whole vocabulary of army swear words, largely a grammatical variant of one in particular, and curse the Germans up hill and down dale, while yet others would join in a popular chorus. One man had snapshots of his family spread out and was showing them to his neighbour; another, a young officer, was reading the New Testament.

Most of the wounded in this ward had received injuries to their legs and were left with the fullest capacity for mental and physical suffering, being obliged to endure without being able to stir an inch, yet feeling in other respects hale and hearty. It was as though they had been nailed alive to the floor boards, but into their torment was brought the comfort made available by another, earlier nailing – that to the Cross – through the gallant and selfless ministration of a padre, who wrote numberless letters for them, kneeling beside mattresses and stretchers, lighting cigarettes, giving out boiled sweets, praying with those who requested, and allowing his hand to be cramped in the vice of their white-knuckled, clenched fists.

Perhaps the greatest burden of endurance was placed on a big, tough glider-pilot sergeant who had had the misfortune to sprain both his ankles very badly when his glider had crash-landed. A sprain is sometimes more disabling than a fracture since bones knit more easily than ligaments, and this man, having been carried from the landing field and brought to this hospital, had lain on his mattress ever since; a husky, fighting man, a shorn Samson, put out of action without ever having struck or received a blow, until a piece of metal flashing through the window practically severed his right hand from his wrist. And there were others: a man lying face downward because of a wound in his buttock, having his shoulder sliced open as though he had been struck with a razor sharp whip; and the medical orderly, standing over a stretcher, who suddenly collapsed onto the wounded man beneath him, and lay there dead with a hole in the back of his head, until others pulled him off.

Simmons and I crawled round from case to case, as we carried out our duties with an automatic administration of our hands, set smiles on our faces, minds numb and withdrawn, closing our senses against noises, sights and smells in an inward struggle to disregard the circumstances. Throughout the hospital, in the rooms which were exposed, the same scenes were repeated. Outside erupting chaos, inside a brotherhood of suffering and service. Wounded, nurses, orderlies, administrators, padres, doctors all face to face with the same crashing world, all digging down into their deepest sources of endurance and miraculously finding something that answered their purpose.

✳

On the Arnhem road an artillery dual was in progress between our anti-tank guns dug in on the crossroads and an enemy self-propelled gun which had appeared cautiously out of a side-turning a hundred yards up the road, and under the protection of which German were gathered like infantry pilot fish round a marauding shark. The anti-tank gun had got the first shot in, which went across its bows and ploughed into the road, throwing up a large splash of dirt and cobbles. The self-propelled gun had withdrawn sensitively like the horns of a snail and, moving through back gardens, had established itself in a position from which it could advance, fire a shot, and retire again behind the cover of a house. The enemy were too professional to repeat the manoeuvre more than twice from the same place and varied their position, creeping out onto the main road from between different houses, while their infantry sprayed windows with machine gun fire to neutralize the fire from the British who were in possession of some of the houses.

Shells whistled up and down the road, like a moaning, invisible scythe cutting lethal swathes in the air a mere yard or two from the front of the hospital, which lay quivering on the edge of an ever-contracting no man's land as the Germans pressed their attack against the perimeter. The gunners on the crossroads sought desperately to register vital hits with their dwindling supply of shells, and stuck grimly to their position in the face of the most crushing delivery from every kind of weapon pouring upon them. In the houses lightly armed paratroopers, also nursing every round of ammunition, poked rifles and Sten guns out of windows from beneath barricades of furniture and shot economically with all the inherited skill of the British army at the moving but numerous grey targets, who to advance had to expose themselves and who sprang up and wilted like some precocious and fantastic vegetation in the gardens of the Dutch.

As the gap narrowed, the mortars were called off and the combatants became locked in a man-to-man embrace, the arch of the defenders held by the keystone of the anti-tank guns, against which the attackers swung the battering ram of the self-propelled monster. In the hospital it was impossible not to be aware the climax was approaching. For no battle could continue with such ferocity without something giving way. Through the ground-floor windows sudden blemishes and pock-marks could be seen appearing on the walls of adjacent buildings as Spandaus licked at them. As it became evident the main enemy effort was being made here, and the crossroad was bearing the brunt of the attack, Airborne men from less contested sectors of the perimeter were fed in and were sometimes visible, flitting through the shrubbery and woods at the back of the hospital. Soon all pretence at treatment ceased, and wounded and workers lay side by side on the dusty floors waiting with bated breath for the decision.

While the hospital, like a prostrate suppliant, prayed for deliverance from this ordeal and, outside, the men-at-arms of both nations strove to subdue each other, it transpired that a private with a Piat (anti-tank rocket gun) detached himself from a doorway in the third or fourth row back from the main road and started to pick his way carefully through the bushy gardens towards a distant throbbing noise, distinguished by his trained ears from the general mêlée as the straining engines of a German self-propelled. He was from one of the sections switched into the fight from a reserve position, and in his mind now shone nothing else but the exciting and glorious chance that there might fall to him one of the greatest prizes possible to a single-handed soldier. He could hear the unseen engine coughing deep-throatedly not far ahead of him, and the clanking of the tracks as they gained purchase on the road, and he squirmed and wriggled and edged from cover to cover oblivious of any other consideration save that of approaching the monster unseen. The nearer he got the more hazardous it became, owing to increasing concentration of Germans, and he at length found himself pinned down in a small summer-house unable to advance any further, his way barred by a pair of broad grey backs arising like accessory gate-posts from the particular garden to which his stalk had brought him.

He watched them, hoping they would move, his eyes darting this way and that probing for an alternative route to his target, but there seemed no choice between staying where he was or retracing his steps and, of the two, the latter seemed less desirable. Now that he was immobilized in the summer-house he became acutely aware of the precariousness of his position. He had somehow managed to insinuate himself into the thick of the enemy without realizing it, so intent had he been on his quarry, and he was uncomfortably considering his next move when, by one of those freak chances on which sometimes hang great issues, the gun chose that very moment to back away from the main road, baffled by the sizzling fire from the anti-tank guns on the hospital corner. It clanked reversing down the side road, inexorably drawing closer to where the Piat gunner palpitated in the summer-house, until it eventually framed itself for him in the gap between the two Germans, behind whom he was concealed.

Calmly and deliberately he rested the Piat on a window sill and fired his bomb. There was an explosion and a sheet of flame, and the self-propelled rocked to a standstill. He watched fascinated for a split second and then turned and bolted across the garden to the next house, swerving and jinking with the Piat under his arm like a rugby footballer. He just had the edge on the Germans, who took longer to recover from their surprise than he to start his run and, with bullets spattering around him, he reached the cover of the blind side of the building, leaped over a fence into other premises and disappeared through a side door.

At the contested crossroads the fighting did not immediately cease after the gun had been put out of action, but there was an unmistakable slackening of the German effort; a kind of defervescence, with longer periods between the bursts of firing that, after quarter of an hour, had the defences hoping against hope they had repulsed the attack and, before half an hour was up, had given them complete assurance they had done so. The perimeter had held and the hospital was still on the British side of the line. By noon the Medical Corps men were able to emerge from their battered hotel, blinking in the sunlight like troglodytes, to begin the task of surveying and recovering the wounded from the battlefield, and repairing the damage to their own establishment.

Lt-Colonel Marrable, having asked for a situation report from all his officers and NCOs and having had time to digest it, called another conference, held as before in the kitchen. Now that the heavy ballast of immediate danger was thrown overboard, everyone was buoyant in spirit, but fatigue was etched on every face, and while Marrable, as was his wont, sat on the table, most of us slumped down on the floor, leaning against the walls, as we listened wearily to what he had to say.

'Well, chaps,' he began, 'it looks as if we've got a problem or two on our hands. The water mains have had it and the drains are useless. The lavatories are blocked and overflowing, which you have no doubt noticed.' He wrinkled his nose in an expression of disgust. 'Every bit of refuse will have to be carried out to pits which are now being dug out there,' he jerked his head towards the window, 'and everyone able to walk must answer calls of nature in the garden.

Water parties will have to go out to the well and bring back as many jerry-cans full as the situation will allow. Baths, basins and every available receptacle in the building must be filled, if possible before nightfall, and every drop of water must be boiled before it is used for drinking. Sergeant Major tells me we've only enough food in the place for one more meal all round, and forage parties will have to be detailed to go out and bring in what they can.' He paused to light and draw on his pipe. 'I'm afraid some men have been killed this morning and others have died, and there are others in a very bad way who cannot be expected to live much longer. I have been asked by the padre if he may be notified of all on the danger list so that they can be visited. We shall not be able to spare the men just yet to bury the dead and, with the padre's approval, I have selected the garage as a temporary resting place for them.' He paused, stabbed the air several times with his pipe and continued emphatically. 'There's a very great deal to be done, and not least of our difficulties will begin when we are faced with the new influx of wounded from this morning's action which the stretcher parties will soon be bringing in. There are two brighter items of news.' We all perked up. 'Communication has been firmly established with the Second Army. They are definitely through Nijmegen in strength and may even get some units to the ferry tonight. Second, there's a supply drop scheduled for this afternoon. Our immediate future depends, however, on the success of the water and forage parties, and we shall be very short-handed until they get back. The first job in here is to get the sewage out of the place and get it cleaned up. When that's done we'll get a meal round to everyone, and when that's done we'll see how we stand. I'm hoping the enemy has shot his bolt for today and we shall have a long enough respite to get on top of things.' He swung himself off the table. 'Right. That's it.'

We climbed to our feet. Some gathered round Marrable to consult him on various points pertaining to their work while others, including Simmons and myself, dispersed to the various parts of the hospital of which they had charge. In the ward it was a question of where to begin. Plaster dust lay everywhere, on the men lying on the floor, in their hair and moustaches, on the dressings and in the instrument trays. Several hands were raised in request for bedpan or bottle but most of the wounded lay inert, their eyes closed, having succumbed to the desire for sleep which pressed upon everyone when the shooting was over. After the intensive noise there was an uncanny silence, into which Simmons' voice suddenly boomed like a circus master. 'Anybody here got a vacuum cleaner?

The careful division of labour by which the Medical Corps normally organized its work went by the board. Majors, captains and lieutenants seized brooms, shovels, bedpans and buckets alongside the lowliest private, and all joined in a feverish attack against the accumulation of soiled dressings, excreta and plain dirt, which now constituted the greatest danger to health and life. The nauseating smell from the stopped-up lavatories and from septic wounds permeated the whole hospital. The only solution to the sanitary problem was to place buckets in the wards to act as minor reservoirs, which naturally added to the smell, and to carry them out and empty them as they became full. Soluble lysol tablets were used as disinfectant, but the general effect of this was to add what can only be classed as another unpleasant odour to the existing miasma and to draw more attention to the existence of these cess-pits. The wounded had to be dusted and brushed as if they were pieces of furniture, while blankets and removable pieces of clothing were shaken out of the windows.

While I worked, my thoughts turned back to the CCP, the barn, and the experiences I had shared there with Dwyer, Adams and the Dutch nurse. I realized, apart from the nurse, I had seen very little of them and resolved to look them up later and find out how they had been faring. The nurse at this time was occupied with the care of the more seriously wounded in one of the big ground-floor rooms. Here, where the configuration of the building offered the greatest peace and protection, the real battles were being waged for the lives of men terribly injured and fearfully maimed; those with penetrating wounds of the head, chest and abdomen, those with faces shot away, with arms and legs blown off who lay scarcely conscious, while all the reserves of medical skill were pitted against loss of blood, sepsis, fever, delirium, ebbing strength of body and depression of mind. Those who such a short time ago had been in the prime of vigour and health now groaned and sweated and struggled to survive; those too feeble to catch the life-lines thrown to them gradually sank, while the padre knelt beside them striving to ease their passing with prayer and love.

In another part of the building Private Adams, detailed as supernumary clerk to the stores Sergeant, checked off the dwindling supply of medical equipment as it was issued out, and thought it really wasn't very much different from serving in his father's shop in the early part of the blitz. You took cover when you heard one coming, otherwise you just got on with it. He felt he had come down in the world. A captain's clerk was distinctly superior to a sergeant's. The tight little association, of which he had been a contented member in the Battalion, had been blown apart and scattered through the hospital. We were like men having left school, absorbed into a wider organization of life, and feeling almost like strangers at the rare moments when our paths crossed.

Dwyer was leading a section of men out on a foraging party. It was inevitable, with all the other sergeants in the DS fitted into regular jobs for which they had been personally trained, that a displaced person like Dwyer should be given some of the less enviable tasks arising out of the action. Earlier he had been called upon to deal with a fire that broke out in a crashed vehicle. This vehicle was a kind of light van, previously commandeered and used by the Germans, which in swerving to avoid a pot-hole had mounted the pavement and wrapped itself round a tree near reception. When, during the height of the fighting, it caught fire and, burning furiously, began to threaten the hotel, Dwyer with half a dozen orderlies managed to tow it out of harm's way with a chain of toggle ropes attached to the back axle – a manoeuvre involving the utmost hazard, both from the flaming vehicle itself and the flying missiles of the battle.

Now he was off on a more dangerous assignment still. Foraging for food meant not only exposing one's person in vegetable gardens but also entering houses, and one could not always be certain in advance that they were not occupied by the enemy. In battles of this kind small groups of men would be constantly cut off, obliging them to lie concealed during the hours of daylight, until the advent of darkness gave them the opportunity of readjusting their position. Thus, each house had to be approached with extreme circumspection. If no response came to knocking at the door, an entry had to be forced and the risk taken of finding the enemy lurking in a dark corner with surprise on his side. Immediate advantage had to be taken of the present lull. There was no time for the formal post-engagement report to be circulated to commanders indicating positions held by friend or foe, for no one knew how soon the battle might not be rejoined. Dwyer, in fact, found himself in the position of both forager and reconnoitrer, with instructions to bring back a detailed report of any enemy activity he encountered in the neighbourhood.

The shops on either side of the Arnhem road had long since been stripped of their edibles, so he set off in a southerly direction through the woods and gardens towards the river. He was followed by a man carrying a large Red Cross flag, which he held aloft and waved conspicuously whenever the tenancy of a building seemed in doubt.

The first house they entered was empty, and they searched it from top to bottom without collecting more than a bag of lentils and a bad fright for Dwyer who, on opening a door to one of the upper rooms, was nearly precipitated into space, as the floor, having collapsed, sloped away to ground level like a chute. The second house was occupied. Incredible as it may seem, in the middle of all the crashing madness, there was a family attempting to lead a sane day-to-day existence. In the cellar, lit by two guttering candles, an elderly couple were sitting on a trestle-bed, the woman knitting, the man playing with a little girl who was trying to extract something out of his closed fist. At first, owing to the gloom, Dwyer only saw these three but as he turned to go, not wishing to disturb them, he saw another bed in a further corner and on it, to his astonishment, was lying an Airborne soldier asleep, while a young woman at his side was washing bandages in a basin standing on a rickety table.

Dwyer went over to the man and took in his appearance with a practised glance, noting a good colour, quiet peaceful breathing and a blood-stained bandage under the shirt by the left collar bone. He raised his eyebrows in a question to the girl who, in halting English, explained that the soldier had taken refuge there the day before, not having been in a fit condition, and had spent the morning watching at an upstairs window with his rifle, while the battle raged round the house. Now, exhausted by his vigil, he had gone to sleep. Dwyer explained his own mission and found himself embarrassed by the generosity of these Dutch people, who begged him to take some of their food for the wounded, in spite of their own need, and made him feel he ought to give them the miserable bag of lentils that hardly seemed worth keeping anyway. Before leaving he gave them the position of the hospital, and the girl said she would try to get the soldier over to it during the night.

As they were about to enter the third house, they heard the growing sound of low-flying aircraft. They paused on the threshold and looked in the direction from which the sound was coming, and very quickly caught sight of squadrons of Dakotas plunging through the low cloud layer like a school of whales. Sporadic firing, continuing in distant places, now intensified and built up into a formidable barrage of anti-aircraft fire. Every weapon on the ground held by the enemy seemed to be opening up, and the Dakotas flew through a display of pyrotechnics that would not have disgraced a Brock's benefit night. Dwyer and his men stood looking up open-mouthed, mesmerized by the sight, until a sudden rattle of spent shrapnel descending round them made them dash for cover inside the house, forcing an entrance through a lower window. From there they craned their heads out watching the drop. Unfortunately most of the planes passed majestically overhead without discharging their cargo, and only a handful of coloured parachutes came floating down in the vicinity. One Dakota, as it flew through the barrage, suddenly lurched and black smoke appeared from an engine. Although beginning to lose height it never faltered, even when the black smoke had turned to red flames.

In the silence after their departure Dwyer led his party out into the woods where the nearest parachute had landed and found a hamper, full of clothing and blankets. It was not the food they had been hoping for, but was better than nothing and they decided to wheel it back to the DS on the collapsible trolley they had brought with them, before resuming their forage.

The search for food met with a certain amount of success, including the capture of two live sheep quickly despatched, and the water parties were making uninterrupted journeys to and from the well. One or two of the supply containers had been recovered packed with food, and one forager had discovered two sacks of oatmeal. There was enough to ensure that the hospital had enough in the way of porridge and stew for another twenty-four hours.

Gradually the concerted efforts of the Medical Corps in the cleaning-up process bore fruit and by late afternoon, in the absence of any further move by the enemy, it had been possible to restore some semblance of order. The building, especially the upstairs part, was seriously damaged, although the mortar bombs that had exploded on the roof had not penetrated the ceilings of the first floor. Considering the vulnerable position of the hospital, direct hits had not been excessive, and the Germans were given credit for having tried to avoid it since they knew the use to which the hotel was being put from their previous occupancy, and that it contained some of their own wounded men.

After the strenuous work of the afternoon the main preoccupation was with fatigue, which can set in suddenly when absorption in work ceases, knocking strength from the legs, as a single hammer blow knocks the wedge from a partly sawn-through tree and brings it crashing down. There was little inclination on anyone's part for conversation, for it was best to leave unsaid the thoughts universal in every mind. Where was the Second Army? When would they come? How much longer could this go on? What had happened at the Bridge? Men fell asleep in odd corners as soon as the evening meal of porridge had been distributed. There was a short social half-hour in the kitchen where the officers and Dutch ladies shared a brew of the now ever-weakening tea, and an economical pull on one of the dwindling number of cigarettes: a good-night ceremony to round off the day that had become a firmly established feature of this fantastic community life.

This night it was the turn of others for the cupboard under the stairs and Simmons and I betook ourselves to the recovery ward where there was straw on the floor, whether as an absorbent or for warmth I did not care. We found unoccupied spaces as far from the windows as possible and lay down among the patients. My last memory of that day is of mice rustling in the straw.

Friday 22 September

At the break of day which, for the German purpose of battle, habitually seemed synonymous with six o'clock, I was still lying in an untidy heap in the recovery ward. I had not even bothered to remove my tie but had flopped wearily onto the floor and, as the only civilized concession to the ritual of going to bed, had taken off my boots and covered myself with a blanket, resting my head as usual on my haversack. Now I dreamed of a knocking and a noise like the rumbling of thunder, that in my stupor I interpreted as someone demanding urgent entry from some kind of storm. I was not ready to awake, the repair to the ravages of fatigue still demanding several hours for completion. Simmons and I had sniffed around like dogs for a resting place the night before, and finding one had dropped into it without notifying control point where we were. We had, in consequence, been overlooked in the general awakening of all officers carried out by an orderly corporal before the lifting of darkness. Consciousness slowly returned as I groped in my mind for an explanation of the noise, until with a click the penny dropped and I was on my feet, shouting at Simmons, and racing into the hall towards the control point like a homing pigeon.

My reaction to the bombardment was one of anger and exasperation. As I laboured up the stairs to our ward, unshaven and breakfastless, I was calling the Germans every name I could think of under the sun. The whole futility of their war seemed epitomized in the morning flight of mortar bombs, screaming and thumping their way blindly into the ground outside, the whole stupid fallacy that one race could ever permanently dominate another by force of arms. Where, I asked myself rhetorically, did they ever get the idea they could impose their mastery on Europe, with all the ridiculous nonsense about their historical destiny as a master race? Where had they got the idea they could rule by fear? Every nation in the world has produced men that could fight bravely and die bravely, who would rather be dead than submit to an alien domination. Fear only works up to a point. After a time it is possible to get used to it, and familiarity in the end breeds contempt. And as for glory; glory in the last analysis only boils down to a conquest of self, military glory to a supremely unselfish disregard of pain and death in the face of the enemy; but there are other kinds of enemy that enable this to be practised without war. Who would say that the act of killing is glorious, of bereaving, of maiming, of destroying other people's property? I thought, as I laid my hand on the handle of the ward door, that anyone interested in starting a war should come and spend an hour or two among the suffering wounded, observe German and British lying helpless side by side, indistinguishable in their bravery, paying the grisly price. I kicked the door open savagely. The power-crazy don't care. They don't care what they start and they don't know how to stop it.

I was on my own in the ward to begin with as Simmons, the acknowledged expert in the art of improvisation, had been detained by Marrable and given the task of organizing the construction of splints out of wood taken from the wreckage, which especially abounded in the attic. The Thomas's splints, brought in with the Field Ambulance, had long since run out, and the problem of immobilizing fractured femurs was now one on which Simmons was asked to exercise his ingenuity.

The NCO, who had been on duty in the ward during the hours of darkness, handed me the night book in which he had entered details of drugs administered, temperature, pulse and respiration rate, together with any relevant comments on the condition of each patient. I ran a practised eye over these details while the barrage thundered outside.

'This man's temperature has risen rather sharply,' I commented.

'Yes, sir, he's got a lot of swelling in his leg I don't like the look of much either,' replied the orderly.

I studied the case history, transferring salient details into my own case note-book which I always carried around on my person in case the ward record should become a casualty: 'Gunshot wound right leg with compound fracture of tibia and fibula, wound toilet [removal of dirt, clothing fragments, bits of metal and cutting away of hopelessly damaged tissue] and above knee plaster of Paris splint at 1930 hours yesterday, two tablets of sulphanilamide 4-hourly since admission. Not in too much pain until late last night when required

112

¼ grain of morphia.'

'Right, Corporal, I'll take a look at it. You go off now and get some beauty sleep.'

The Corporal withdrew, the corners of his mouth pulled down disdainfully at the euphemistic description applied to what promised to be another uncomfortable morning spent in a dark, dank, thudding cellar, trying to reach sleep through a barrier of alertness, unable to shut out the thought of what was going on overhead. Not much beauty, not much sleep; but still it was relatively safe down there and he thankfully made tracks for it.

The wounded man was one of those unfortunates lying near the window. The mattress Simmons and I had thrust into the lower part of it still gave a certain amount of protection, but the stuffing was coming out in places where it had absorbed metal fragments, and it did nothing to mitigate the noise which battered at the nerves with a threat of sudden injury or disaster. An increase in the relation of whistles to crashes indicated that a target rather more distant than the Hartenstein area was receiving the brunt of the enemy softening-up process. Shells were passing overhead in an unending stream while, compared with yesterday, the explosions in the immediate vicinity were reduced; but this was an academic consideration.

Many of the wounded had been lying in this room for the best part of five days, their resistance and vitality gradually being sapped by pain, toxaemia and semi-starvation. Colour had drained from their faces from which, owing to the difficulties, it had not recently been possible to remove the stubble. Their eyes were red-rimmed and bloodshot, and there were few now who could summon a complete show of indifference to the bombardment. They stared at the ceiling as if trying to follow the track of each missile, and with every crump they twitched and started. They were beyond defeat because they could not run away, and though they might not be able to control their bodies they did control their tongues: no complaints, no accusations, no squeals, just grim, silent endurance, save from those who could not suppress an involuntary groan when I had to handle their wounds.

I examined the man's thigh above the upper rim of the plaster of Paris splint that encircled his leg down to the foot, and with careful fingers palpated a puffy swelling under the skin. It had a curious feel like well-aerated dough. I began to worry as my fingers sank with almost a crackle into what should have been the firm flesh of the thigh. It evoked some text-book memory which I sought intently to

113

recall. Some instinct implanted by past medical training prompted me to put my nose closer to the plaster, and then the diagnosis leapt into my mind, gas gangrene. This was serious; as far as I had heard, the first case we had had. I made a rapid assessment of the man's general condition, drew a blue mark on the skin with a coloured pencil to denote the upper limit of the swelling, and then lost no time in descending to the hall and informing Marrable of my diagnosis.

'If you're sure of that,' Marrable said, 'we'll have to get a surgeon up to look at it.'

One of the then usual forms of treatment for gas gangrene, which is caused by a germ that multiplies in the absence of oxygen, was, as well as administering serum, re-excising the wound and making incisions to let the gas out and the air in. It was always a desperate business, since the infection spreads silently without betraying its presence until the gas has formed, and often an urgent amputation is required to control the spread.

The arrival of the CO and the surgeon at his side filled the patient with alarm and apprehension. 'What is it, sir?' he asked, raising himself on his elbows and looking anxiously at the surgeon as he prodded his thigh.

'It's nothing,' replied Marrable. 'We were rather proud of this splint and wanted to show it off to the Major.'

'That's right. It's a very good one,' the latter said, 'but I'm afraid it will have to come off. It's such a good fit it's getting too tight. The circulation gets a bit sluggish when you lie about like this, and the limb swells.'

The man subsided back again, the lines of anxiety easing from his face. 'It feels all right,' he said, 'it was throbbing last night but has stopped now.'

'Nevertheless,' pursued the surgeon, 'I'm afraid the plaster will have to come off and we shall have to give you some injections to try to get the swelling down.'

As I escorted them to the door the surgeon said to me, 'It'll be touch and go whether we can save his leg. There may be a chance with the serum, and it'll be a good opportunity to test all they've claimed for this penicillin stuff. Will you give him some of both and bring him down to the theatre as soon as possible.'

I returned to the soldier's side, who shot out a claw-like hand and plucked at my battle dress.

'They wasn't fooling was they, sir? There isn't anything serious wrong?'

'No, not yet,' I parried, 'but there might be if we don't get the plaster off. So best not to worry about it. Let's get on with it. I've got to give you those injections now to help get the swelling down.'

I consulted my treatment book, and prepared and administered 20,000 units of penicillin intravenously and 70,000 units intramuscularly, together with 7½cc anti-gas serum intravenously and 22cc intramuscularly, and noted them down in my own case book. I also gave him half a grain of morphia as a premedication for his anaesthetic.

While the soldier lay on the table in the theatre, mercifully unconscious, I continued the rounds of the patients upstairs. The character of the work was changing. When the ward had been filled with newly wounded there was an urgency to get them all seen to in a surgical sense, to control bleeding, extract bullets and shell fragments, cut away devitalized tissue, set fractures and immobilize damaged limbs in plaster. Now the floor space was entirely occupied by men who had been thus attended to and who required but a twice-daily examination to ensure that all was going well, coupled with the nursing that tended to the wants of nature and the maintenance of strength.

On us now devolved the far more difficult task of doctoring minds. Difficult because it demanded feats of imagination and inventiveness that made the practical management of wounds look like child's play. The greatest need of the wounded now was for reassurance, constant and convincing reassurance that the battle outside was going well, and that they would soon be gathered up into the arms of the Second Army and be borne swiftly to the base hospitals for the rest and quiet and further expert treatment they knew they needed. During the bombardment, therefore, I remained in the ward, more from the principle of showing the flag than for purposes of treatment, trying to appear nonchalant, squatting in turn by the side of the men and carrying on elaborate conversations of any optimistic or humorous nature that would come to mind; that is to half my mind, for with the other I was listening to the noises off, endeavouring to translate them into military meaning, to discover whether the enemy was building up into another attack like the day before and, by the quality of the return fire from the Airborne forces, to estimate our chances of holding.

The prospect of being retaken prisoner I regarded with moderate equanimity. It was not only possible but probable, in view of the peripheral position of the hospital, that the Germans would again engulf us in one of their flooding waves of attack; but I felt reasonably confident that an ebb could set in, as had happened before, and leave us again high and dry. Nothing could at present shake off the feeling of overall Allied invincibility, based, not unsoundly, on our unchecked and relentless progress since Alamein and, especially, on the breath-taking speed of our advance since the break-out in Normandy. It was obvious to the meanest intelligence that the days of Hitler's Reich were numbered, that the regime, whose name would for ever be linked with the vile brutality of the concentration camps, of racial persecution and arrogant disregard for the rights of the individual, would soon itself be destroyed and, since the Anglo-Saxon race has a tolerant and forgiving nature, its survivors would no doubt receive an impartial justice they would in no way have extended to others, had the position been reversed. For the war was between two concepts of greatness: the concept of Hitler and his spiritual predecessors that greatness lay in the pride of physical power, an edifice raised on the bowed backs of people who cringed in fear, and the concept that has caught and held the imagination of liberty-loving people since one Man washed the feet of his disciples two thousand years ago, that true greatness is inseparable from humble service and the test of a leader is whether he looks upon his position as a God-given opportunity to serve his fellow men, not as a haughty eminence from which to compel them to serve him.

But, even as I strained my ears at the runs and trills of small-arms fire that embellished the main theme of mortaring, the unexpected happened. As though a conductor had dropped his baton there suddenly fell a silence, in which the soulful whisper of a rising wind could be heard crepitating through the dry autumnal leaves; a silence that generated a sinister tension of expectation as to what might be going to happen next. After gazing in statuesque surprise at the window for some minutes I exclaimed, irrelevantly, in an unnaturally loud voice, 'I say. I do believe it's going to rain.'

As the silence continued and we all listened and waited, I, battle-wary though I had become, was fain to expose my person in order to satisfy my curiosity and, leaning out of the window over the ragged mattress, I searched the shrubbery and woods for signs of activity. But there were none. For some reason, best known to themselves, the enemy had halted their attack, and the Airborne men, albeit no doubt suspicious and mistrustful, were content to withhold their fire from none too certain targets when every single round of ammunition was as precious as gold. The minutes ticked by without a word being spoken or a shot being fired until, at last, a wounded Sergeant, unable to contain his hopes any longer, voiced a thought that I must admit had crossed my mind also. 'Isn't this what you would expect if the lads across the river had got into Arnhem?' The excitement in his voice increased. 'Wouldn't the Jerries have to make a sudden about-turn to protect their rear?'

The casual words worked like yeast in a vat, and soon eager bubbles of conversation burst out all over the room.

'What do you think, sir?' asked one of the men.

I was not sure what to think. I knew I should guard against and in no way encourage over-wishful thinking, but it did seem a possibility. I rubbed my unshaven chin.

'It could be,' I said cautiously, 'but you never know what tricks Jerry is going to get up to. I shall believe the Second Army is here only when I can see them. I'll go down and see if they know anything at control.'

In the hall everything looked much as usual. A signalman sat behind the counter with earphones on his head, and wounded lay along the walls. Orderlies walked past in pursuit of their duties and there was none of the excitement in the air I had left upstairs. I was told the CO was in the kitchen so I made my way there, feeling a great sense of anticlimax, more than enhanced when Marrable, taking one look at me, said, before I had time to mention what was in my mind, 'You look as if you could do with a shave.'

'Yes, sir,' I answered, crestfallen, 'I was caught on the hop this morning.' Then smiling apologetically and remembering my mission I went on, 'Excuse me, sir, but the men upstairs in my ward are expressing a great desire to know the cause of this sudden calm. They've got it into their heads the enemy is on the run because the Second Army has arrived in the town. Is there any news? Do you think there could be any truth in it?'

Marrable took a pull at his pipe. 'There could be. But there is nothing firm to go on. It can only be speculation at this stage. We shouldn't encourage too much optimism. If it is true, we shall know soon enough. Tell them I will let everyone know as soon as there is any definite news one way or the other.'

He must have seen something in my face for he added gently, 'I am hoping and wishing for it to be true as much as any of you.'

I thanked him, glad I was not bearing the burden of his responsibility but at the same time hating to have to return to the ward, as it

117

were, empty-handed. But I breezed in, taking the non-commital line. 'As I rather expected there's no definite news. We'll have to wait and see. There'll be a brew-up directly which shouldn't be quite as bad as mortar bombs.'

I fingered my chin again and turned to the orderly. 'I'm going to get a shave. Keep an eye on things.' I went back to the kitchen to a bucket of water and dipped in my mess tin. After shaving I wiped the soap scum from the surface of the water in the tin and poured it back in the bucket. All the time I had been listening, and still the only sound was of the rising wind, blowing in gusts and driving dead leaves and rubbish into corners.

To me, no less than to others in the hospital, the ensuing hours were as trying in their own way as any that had gone before. At first, while we all expected the enemy to resume his offensive at any time, it was relatively easy to subdue hopes of an early rescue by the Second Army, but as the hours passed and the enemy showed no further sign of activity an irrepressible wave of optimism spread like a slow fire through the building, until at last even the least com-bustible, including the CO, was affected by it, and the atmosphere became charged with an almost hysterical current of expectation.

Those wounded, who had hitherto lain inert, husbanding their strength and fighting their pain, now eagerly searched the face of every orderly or doctor as they passed for confirmation of the news they waited for. Raising themselves feebly and propping themselves on an elbow, they would survey the scene for a few moments and exchange a word with their neighbours, before letting themselves drop back momentarily exhausted by their efforts. Men of the Medical Corps gathered in animated knots, as good-humoured as though they were already getting ready to go on leave, while some of the officers congregated outside the service door by the garage gazing intently down the road to Arnhem, something they would have considered as suicidal the previous morning.

Across the road could be seen some Airborne soldiers gazing at them through barricaded windows, raising their fingers in the 'V' sign. Even the desolation of the torn-up pavé, angulated tram-lines, trailing telephone wires and battered, windowless and in many cases roofless houses, failed to clip by one pinion the wings of their soaring spirits. Although it had begun to rain and the sky was overcast, they, we, stood there enthusiastically in bemused expecta-tion of seeing a British armoured column appear at any instant on the horizon of the long straight road, ready to cheer, already mentally throwing caps into the air, longing and hoping for the end of the ordeal, eager for the victory which had been so long in coming. Major Frazer had other thoughts: the arrival of the rain and the possibility it offered for replenishing the water supply. While we were standing about outside he was busy organizing collection of rain-water from the gutter piping.

For ten, twenty minutes, perhaps half an hour we clustered on our happy pinnacle of wishful thinking and then, with a feeling of anticlimax, not because we had ceased to believe in the prospect of relief but because it had not come just when we had told ourselves it should, we began to disperse.

'It would take them some time to secure the Bridge and consolidate their position in the town,' suggested Simmons.

'Yes, and remember,' said another, 'their job is still not so much to relieve us as to destroy the German army. They'll probably move round the town in an encircling movement to pinch off the Jerries between us and them. It is even conceivable that some of them may appear first from the opposite direction!'

'Good heavens,' said Simmons, looking quite startled, 'I hadn't thought of that. In that event they would first make contact with the other side of the perimeter. But if they did we ought to get news of it on the blower.'

'Talking of news,' I entered the conversation with what Marrable had said to me earlier in mind, 'you'd think we would have heard something direct from the Second Army by now if they had managed to cross the Bridge.'

This train of thought was not pleasing, and the officer who had hypothesized the encircling movement was quick to submit an explanation. 'Well, in an operation of this kind surprise is very important. Imagine you're a Jerry. As long as we are on the other side of the Bridge he knows we can only have one thing in mind – to get across it, but once we're over he hasn't an exact clue what we propose to do next. He'll probably expect us to try to link up with the perimeter and put his strongest forces across that line. But we might very well decide differently. We might, for example, even strike due east into Germany with the armour, leaving the infantry to mop up here at their leisure. At all events our High Command is unlikely to risk letting the enemy know their intentions by sending us messages across the ether, code or no code.'

For doctors dressed up as soldiers it was a fair exposition. We felt wiser and nodded in agreement.

I lingered a little longer at the door after the others had gone inside. There was something here, in this corner of the building, that drew me. As I stood looking down the road I had a vague feeling of *déjà vu*. I felt it had some significance as a setting in my life, something like the Examination Hall at Queen Square had been in my student days. I went back into the control point area and immediately bumped into the Dutch nurse. In the mood I was in I felt that, too, had significance, but moods are deceptive. I somehow harboured a feeling of guilt for having passed the whole morning without giving her a thought.

'Hallo,' I said brightly. 'I'm afraid I overslept this morning and missed my chance of seeing you. How have you been getting on?'

'Oh, not so bad, and you?' She betrayed no emotion, speaking with the flat voice of the utterly fatigued.

'Wondering very much what the Germans are up to. It does not seem like them to stop attacking with everything to their advantage, unless it is no longer to their advantage.'

'Do you think then, also, that the liberation army might be in Arnhem?' she asked eagerly. 'It is certainly being rumoured among my people.'

'I think they might be,' I replied cautiously, 'but like everyone else I don't know.'

I extracted a cigarette from my battered tin case and tapped it against the back of my thumb nail. Using it to point to a broken window, through which the rain could be seen slanting down in a steady downpour, I said, 'This is what it is like in England nine days out of ten.'

She stood silently watching it, and then said, 'It rains often in Holland, too.'

'On the just and on the unjust?'

'Sorry?'

'Oh, nothing. I was just quoting. You won't forget, will you, about visiting us when all this is over?'

I started thinking how much I would have given to be back home again just now, a thought no doubt stimulated by the believed proximity of the Second Army, and I launched into a eulogy of my homeland which, blushingly, I discovered too late had been unintentionally patronizing, for the comment she made at the end came drily.

'You do not think much of other countries then.'

'Oh, please don't misunderstand me.' I hastened to repair the damage. 'This is the first time I've been abroad. I . . . I . . . kind of expected the places to look different but the people on our side to be similar. It is impossible for us who haven't been occupied by a foreign power for nine centuries to understand what it must have been like for you these last four years. We just could not conceive it happening, but we would simply expect everybody to resist to the utmost and, as we never praise anyone for doing what is expected of them, only if they do more, I hope you will take it as a compliment if I say we do seem as nations to be similar in every way, and what you and your friends have done for us here deserves our highest praise.'

It was her turn to blush. 'Oh, no,' she said, 'it is not more than you should have expected.'

There was an embarrassed silence, and not knowing quite what to say next I changed the subject. 'Have you seen anything of Sergeant Dwyer today?'

'Only a glimpse. He came in earlier today bringing a wounded man from reception for a blood transfusion.'

'It seems a very long time since we were all together in the barn,' I said, 'a very long time.' I looked round the resuscitation ward to where we had strolled while we had been talking. 'Are you particularly busy?'

'No, not especially.'

'Shall we go and find him to see how he is while it's still peaceful?'

Dwyer had, after the bombardment ceased, spent the morning on another outdoor job in charge of a section of stretcher-bearers, answering the call of the runners sent to enlist their aid on behalf of the casualties arising from the bombardment. These casualties were heaviest among those holding defensive positions in slit trenches in the open. To the west of the Schoonoord, where the shops ceased, the terrain was sprinkled with large villas set in wooded gardens and did not offer the same degree of cover as the more tightly packed buildings to the east. The troops had of necessity to be concentrated at important points of defence, and there was an inevitable steady drain of casualties from the wicked mortaring and automatic fire to which they were subjected. The plans for their swift collection, so well exemplified on the dropping zone and in the earlier phases of the battle, had gone up in the smoke of the jeeps. It now depended on the slow, jolting carry of tired, grimy stretcher bearers, who lurched and staggered with their groaning burdens over the torn-up, cratered ground, not infrequently stumbling and falling from sheer fatigue. Any of the wounded who had two good legs and were still conscious walked to the hospital or divisional aid post for treatment and, if at the end of that were able to fire a gun, walked back again to their slit trenches.

A time like this, free from the enemy interference, was a Godsend. Dwyer and his bearers were answering calls for help non-stop, and it was as a familiar bunched-up figure, plodding along the road, that we first sighted him from the littered threshold of reception. Our brief partnership in action had cemented my regard for him and seeing him now caused me a feeling of sadness for the pass to which the Battalion and the old order of things had come. The rain ran off his rimless parachute helmet on to his face in a steady trickle. Every now and then he protruded his lower lip and sucked the moisture off his stubbly moustache. His eyes were sunk into his face, and he seemed to be looking into the far distance as he drove his tired legs over the ground. On reaching reception and seeing me and the nurse, he drew himself up into a brief salute and then leant against a wall, directing the bearers to deposit their load gently within. He had done a lion's share of the carrying, and wanted, I had no doubt, nothing so much as to take his boots off and lie with his feet propped up until the fatigue ran out of them. He took off his helmet and mopped his face with a dirty handkerchief, and summoning a smile, he said, 'Whew! Couldn't half do with a pint, sir.'

I was still lost in the thoughts of the old Battalion life that the sight of him had aroused. I was also shocked at the change visible in his appearance. His face seemed all eyes, lined and gaunt, his battle dress was caked with dirt, and he smelled of stale sweat, as indeed did most of us. But the contrast was pointed because in his own dapper way Dwyer had been fanatical about cleanliness, and had been known to put a man on a charge for dirty feet, albeit they had blisters on them the size of half crowns.

'It may not be too long now before you get one,' I said, jerking myself out of my reverie.

'My God, sir,' he said, ignoring my remark and pursuing his own train of thought, 'you ought to see the shambles there out by Div HQ. The ground's like a stretch of open-cast mining, all slit trenches and bomb holes. They've just about had it, I reckon. The Hartenstein looks as if it would fall down if you pushed it. They're practically out of ammo and there's precious little grub. This place is a palace compared with that lot.'

'There seems good ground for thinking they won't have to stick it much longer,' I said.

'There may be good grounds here, but all I can say is they don't think so out there,' countered Dwyer gloomily. 'A sergeant I spoke to said they'd all written themselves off. They've seen so many of the lads go. When you've spent the day in a slit trench with your best pal blown open beside you, you don't give a damn. All you want to do is kill Germans. Trouble is, sir, there's not enough left of them to hold on much longer.'

I realized Dwyer had seen things and was speaking about an experience I could not share, and, becoming rather anxious at the effect his words might be having on the nurse, I said with finality, 'Well, it's good to see you. Keep up the good work, Jerry isn't bothering us much at the moment and there must be a good reason for that.'

At two o'clock in the afternoon the sky was mightily rent by the sound of numerous aircraft, and Dakotas of the supply drop again roared overhead, threading their way like wraiths through the rain clouds. They were flying so low it looked as if one could touch them, and the proximity of these comrades-in-arms gave a fresh fillip to the prevailing optimism that was not, except among the more thoughtful, dashed by the defiant and enormous clatter of anti-aircraft fire that sprang up from the Arnhem-ward side of the hospital. Whatever might be the preoccupation of the Germans they were not too busy, or on the defensive, to be debarred from putting up a terrific barrage that took painful toll of the lumbering planes. Unfortunately, in spite of the tenacious courage of the airmen, the greater part of the supplies again failed to fall within the perimeter, and the many spectators from the hospital who rushed out to watch had the chagrin of seeing coloured parachutes opening in huge clusters over the enemy-held territory nearer the town.

When the last flight had passed over and the anti-aircraft fire had died away forage parties once more went out to recover what they could. Water supplies had already been replenished from the gutter pipes and well, and more men were available to scour the woods and gardens for supplies. Some useful medical equipment was recovered and, although the hospital search parties found little in the way of food, we were saved from serious deprivation by the generosity of the fighting men, who brought in as much as they could spare from their own gleanings.

The medical work went on uninterruptedly and once again some order was restored in the building, wards being cleaned and swept, the overdraft of treatments caught up with, and the necessity for frantic improvisation for the time being removed. Expectation of relief remained high, the failure of the Second Army to put in an appearance balanced by the failure of the enemy to resume their attack.

Later in the evening events suddenly moved with a drama that could scarcely have been credited had it not been true. Some of us were having a brew of tea and a cigarette, informally gathered at the control point to which everybody tended to gravitate in spare moments in case there should be any news. The patients were just being put down for the night, the nurses and orderlies making their last sanitary rounds. Padres had said evening prayer, the light was beginning to go, earlier than usual owing to the overcast sky, and we officers were discussing among ourselves the places where we would sleep.

Suddenly there was a hubbub down the passage past the kitchen leading to the service side-door, and a loud voice was heard shouting in Dutch. We, poised mugs in hand, turned as one in the direction of the shouting and immediately a man in civilian clothes rushed into the hall, repeating wildly, now in English, 'The Sherman tanks are coming!'

The Dutch ladies on hearing his voice quickly appeared on the scene, and the Dutchman, for so he proved to be, broke into voluble explanations, again in Dutch, all the while gesticulating and laughing. From the knot of officers Marrable detached himself and restrained the Dutchman with one hand, while beckoning to the lady who owned the hotel with the other, 'Steady on, now. Take it slowly,' he said. 'What's all this about?'

The Dutchman jabbered at the lady, the lady jabbered at the Dutchman and the CO stood lighting his pipe impassively, waiting for them to calm down. Eventually the lady, visibly excited, said, 'This man is from the Oosterbeek underground. He says he has information that Sherman tanks of the Second Army have entered Arnhem and are coming in this direction.'

Marrable looked incredulous.

'Wait a minute,' he said, 'let's get this straight. Say all that again.'

'This man,' the lady persisted, 'says that the underground in Arnhem has passed it on to the group here that Sherman tanks of the Second Army have entered Arnhem and are coming in this direction.'

'Who is he?' Marrable questioned. 'How am I to know he is genuine?'

'He is known to me personally. He was the owner of a chemist's shop. Everybody in Oosterbeek knows him.' She turned to the other ladies for confirmation. They all nodded in emphatic agreement. 'He can be trusted absolutely.'

There was a pause. Then Marrable turned, took his pipe out of his mouth and said to the signals orderly behind the counter, 'Make to Div. HQ. I am informed by the Dutch underground that tanks of the Second Army are approaching on the Arnhem-Utrecht axis.'

As he gave this order there was a hushed silence and his voice could be heard by everyone in the hall, and by some beyond it. When he had finished there was pandemonium. A spontaneous burst of cheering was started in the hall and quickly spread through the whole hospital. Medical personnel ran out into the road leaping for joy and embracing each other in the manner of footballers when they have scored a goal. The CO shook the man by the hand and handed him his mug of tea. The strains of 'Roll out the Barrel' once more rose from the battered piano, and the rafters, what was left of them, rang with delirious voices.

The excitement was still at its height when, almost unnoticed, a small man, with a grey, dusty face, in full, begrimed battle order, and a Sten gun slung over his shoulder, came in through the front door straight into the hall. He looked quizzically at our group, and someone tapped the CO on the shoulder. Marrable looked round, hastily took the pipe from his mouth, and stood to attention.

'Good evening, sir,' he said in a flat voice.

'Cut out the formalities, Arthur,' the other said. 'I want to speak to you quickly and privately.'

Silence had descended upon the scene, and we all stood to attention as Marrable led his visitor to the operating room, which was at present not being used. As soon as they had disappeared, the Babel broke out again.

'Wonder what the hell the Brig. wants?' said Simmons, voicing the question in all our minds. 'He doesn't look too happy.'

I was thinking he looked like somebody from another world. His appearance fully armed and so unheralded filled me with apprehension. I felt in my bones Brigadier Hackett had not come merely to boost our morale, although this was a legitimate and important reason for the visitation of a senior officer. Colonel Warrack, the senior Medical Officer in the Division, was often with us and we felt better for it. He had, in fact, been in the building when the enemy made their first break-in, and had avoided recognition and premature capture by removing his badges of rank and occupying himself as a ward orderly.

The reason for the Brigadier's visit was the subject of universal debate and at first the consensus opinion was that he must have come to brief the CO for the arrival of the relieving forces. But, as the time ticked away and they remained closeted together, adherence to this view began to wither. One of the orderlies, who had passed by the theatre window on his way to deposit rubbish in the pits dug in the garden, reported that he had observed them deep in conference over a map spread out on the operating table. They had looked very serious and not at all as if about to celebrate a victory. While orderlies and others gradually dispersed to their duty stations, a hard core of officers remained in the hall with the Dutchman and the ladies, waiting the outcome of the conference in the theatre.

When at last they emerged the Brigadier shook Marrable by the hand, shot a brief look and grim smile in our direction and hurried through the door back into the world outside. With a raise of his eyebrows and a jerk of his head the CO signalled the group to follow him, and led us into the kitchen. His face forewarned us that the purpose of the Brigadier's visit had not been pleasant. I knew in my heart that the news was bad but when, at last, the CO disclosed it, the reality was a shock to us all.

'I'll come straight to the point,' said Marrable. 'Those tanks are not Shermans but, as we should have guessed, Germans, and it is thought there may be a brigade of them approaching this particular section of the perimeter down the Arnhem road. The Brigadier thinks they may even attack tonight, at any moment; that they may think they have such overwhelming superiority as to overcome their dislike of darkness. There's absolutely no confirmation that the Second Army is even within striking distance of the Bridge. The mistake our Dutch friends made is most unfortunate but quite understandable. Messages are passed on the underground from mouth to mouth, and the real wonder is their information up to now has been so accurate. You'll appreciate, gentlemen, that this Dressing Station lies in direct line of advance between those tanks and Divisional Headquarters. West of here the country is more open and the tanks more vulnerable, and the Brigadier thinks he may be able to contain them as we have recovered more Piats from the supply drop. But, whichever way you look at it, the immediate prospects for us are extremely grim. Every inch of the enemy advance, when it comes, will be contested. It is possible the tanks will be stopped before they get here, but there's more than a fifty-fifty chance we shall be overrun. I am sorry to have to tell you this,' he paused to re-light his pipe and take a long draw before continuing, while we just froze where we were, hanging on his words and waiting for him to continue, 'it is very hard for all of us, but better we should know about it in advance than be taken by surprise. I want all arms, brought into this building by the wounded, removed immediately and placed in the garage. We aren't allowed to have them in a hospital by the Geneva Convention and the Germans will be in no mood to make allowances. If they reoccupy us we must carry on exactly as before, carry on with the medical work as if they did not exist. The outcome of this battle is not yet decided and although our position is serious it is by no means hopeless. Infantry from the Second Army are hoping to get through to the ferry tonight. It may yet be possible to inject reinforcements over the river and save the bridgehead. I do not want anybody to leave this building without orders, or to expose themselves unnecessarily at windows or doors. We must do nothing to embarrass the defence. A watch will be kept through the night and a roster of duty will be drawn up. Right. Sorry, chaps. That's it.'

The CO did not wait for questions, but swung himself off the kitchen table and out of the door as soon as he had finished speaking. The reversal of fortune had been so total that comment seemed superfluous. There was nothing to say, only duty to be done, and we dispersed quietly to carry out our distasteful and bitter task of informing the rest of the hospital.

One hour later the occupants of the battered building waited, in silence as profound as the darkness, finally disposed and ready for whatever lay ahead. Duty orderlies sat quietly at their candle-lit tables, completing case notes and measuring out drugs for the night. Cigarettes from odd corners of the floor glowed as the wounded sought solace from their predicament, and from strategic positions watchful eyes gazed eastwards, towards the faint glow that lit up the sky over Arnhem – reflection of the burning buildings, testifying to the intensity with which that bone was being contested.

To me it seemed yet again my senses were all concentrated in my ears. The less I heard the more I strove to hear, while the smallest background noises in the hospital, the whispers, coughs, footsteps on the bare floor, assumed exasperating proportions. The silence outside had a wearing quality, like water dripping on a stone. While neither I, nor any of the others wished it to be broken by sounds of an enemy advance, the longer it continued, the more frayed the nerves became, until a point was reached when anything seemed preferable to the excruciating suspense of waiting. Would they attack? They seldom did at night. Yet so long as the perimeter held and the ferry crossing remained in our hands, the chance of re-inforcement and of turning the tables on the enemy was that much greater. I could almost feel the sense of urgency that must be possessing the Germans, feeling it as a black pressure on my own last flicker of hope for the outcome. I had no more illusions about the realities of war, no more feelings of not being totally involved, of being a spectator on the touch-line. I was part of it and it was part of me. The prodigality of that last emotional spree, when it had seemed there might yet be an awakening from the bad dream, had scraped the bottom of the barrel clean of illusion. I faced the truth of the situation quite dispassionately, determined, if humanly possible, to survive but quietly knowing I would be able, if the time came, to accept the limitations my rank and duty placed on my freedom of action.

Slowly the minutes ticked away. Another hour passed and nothing happened. Desire for sleep began to blunt the sharp edge of alertness. Surreptitiously men began to go to their resting places, leaving only those on duty at their posts. Down in the cellar the ladies were already huddled together on mattresses, far beyond concern. Whispers gave way to snores, footsteps to the rustling adjustments of resting bodies, and at last Marrable, who had been sitting in the control point behind the counter like a sphinx betrayed only by the aroma of his pipe, spoke into the darkness, 'I don't believe they'll come tonight. We may as well turn in. No point in wearing ourselves out for nothing.'

To go to bed for Simmons and myself meant nothing more than to remove ourselves from the floor of the hall, where we had been clustered uncomfortably with other officers round the control point, to the floor of somewhere less crowded. The cupboard under the stairs was now the prize billet but we had had our turn, and we once again sought the straw in the resuscitation ward. But this afforded us no refuge, having been filled up during the early part of the day with newly wounded, and eventually we lit on a space on the floor of the operating theatre where our surgical association had first truly begun. Although it had now stopped raining the air was very dank and the room, with its gaping windows, grew progressively colder, making the night a chill vigil of restless discomfort after a short period of thankful sleep.

Saturday 23 September

It was a few minutes after one o'clock in the morning when I first awoke, cramped and shivering, a chill draught impinging on my forehead, the only part of me projecting from beneath the blanket. I remembered at once the issues to be decided and, after looking at my watch to establish the time, lay listening to the moan and patter of the wind in the trees. 'They won't come until it's light now,' I thought, taking comfort in the anticipated hours of peace that I believed lay ahead, almost like a re-run of the morning of take-off. I heard someone stir restlessly in another part of the room, and wondered if he might be lying awake as I was, but I had no desire to be communicative only, if possible, to enjoy a little more sleep before the dawn of the new day. My thoughts drifted from their moorings into brief dreams of other places, until the cold woke me up again.

In the early hours of the morning it became obvious that further sleep was impossible, and I resolved to get up and join the officer on watch. I had been lucky in not being included in the roster for this duty and, although my degree of fatigue coupled with the shortage of food made complete recovery of fitness and strength out of the question, the short sleep had done me good. I stepped over the apparently sleeping bodies of my companions of the night, one or two of whom stirred briefly, and went into the hall. The officer of the watch then on duty sat at the control point, his arms folded across his chest and his head nodding. I touched him on the shoulder.

'How much longer do you estimate it is before dawn?' I asked, after he had opened his eyes and flashed me a tired grin of recognition.

'About an hour and a half I'd say. You'll find some of the chaps in the kitchen. The CO's been prowling about for the last hour.

There'll probably be a brew going. I would join them if I were you.'

I followed his advice. There was a single guttering candle throwing an eerie light on to the small number of men grouped round the kitchen range, waiting for the kettle to boil. The night was still as dark as ever, not a glimmer showing from the window high up on the wall. We conversed in low tones, avoiding where possible direct reference to impending events but discussing closely arrangements that might have to be made for the day, arrangements that left no doubt of our resignation to the certainty of an attack and the probability of recapture. The scalding tea, which by now in reality had become a scarcely disguised drink of hot water, had its usual beneficial effect of chasing chill out of limbs and, to some extent, out of hearts.

'We'll have to have reveille in a quarter of an hour,' observed Marrable, 'in case they spring a surprise on us and start before daylight. We'll get a hot drink round to everyone and, as far as the officers are concerned, we'll all have a shave.'

The CO's insistence on our daily shave might appear irksome under the circumstances, but it was freely acknowledged by us all that the effort was worthwhile in terms of morale, and especially important if we were going to have to confront the enemy. I tried hard not to think ahead, since the only result of so doing was a disagreeable coldness of feeling somewhere below the diaphragm. I was now much better practised at control of attention and managed to compartmentalize my mind tolerably well and concentrate on what was at hand. I deliberately refrained from glancing at my watch. I wrapped myself in a self-spun cocoon of indifference, but a cocoon whose brittleness was as of glass and which shattered into a thousand pieces when, at the stroke of six, there was the shriek of approaching shells and bombs and the hospital shuddered and shook with the first reverberations of the enemy barrage.

This was a barrage exceeding in ferocity and weight of metal anything we had yet to endure. Even though we had been waiting for it, its suddenness took our breath away. I had been reading my case book and literally jumped out of my chair. Very quickly the crescendo of noise skewered us into awareness of nothing but itself. It was unprecedented, shattering and, when it reached what must, could only be, its zenith, went on up, scaling ever greater heights of intensity as the weapons of destruction multiplied and approached, until the whole world seemed to be falling in ruins about us and life suffocating beneath the debris.

The moulded plaster ceiling of the main ward downstairs shook free from its restraining laths and crashed, in a choking white cloud of rubble, on to the wounded and the orderlies attending them. Those who could scrabbled free, looking as if they had been participants in a pitched battle with bags of flour, only to scatter with shouts of alarm as the chandelier followed the ceiling down, fortunately into the momentarily unoccupied centre of the room. In the operating theatre a tank shell tore a gaping hole in the outside wall and passed upwards through the ceiling exploding, by the grace of God, in a cupboard where the only casualties were some brooms and buckets. But a surgeon happening to be there was knocked unconscious by a piece of brick, and the room became quite untenable.

No one aspired to bravado. Those who were able crouched in the centre of the building, away from the windows, taking advantage of any cover from flying missiles and debris the architecture afforded. The misfortune of those wounded who lay in exposed, dangerous positions was tragic, but there was nowhere else for them to lie, and the impossibility of easing their lot had to be accepted as part of the black fortune of war that blindly takes some and spares others. With the building falling to pieces around us the relative safety of any position was open to question.

For three hours the bombardment continued, not, as our experience was suggesting, of the hospital in particular but of the area in general, the noise of individual weapons gradually merging until, in the ultimate crescendo, it was quite impossible to distinguish one from another. How the fighting units withstood the attack was beyond understanding. The hospital was entirely disabled as far as its ability to function in a medical sense was concerned. As casualties were sustained a shout would go up and we would rush to carry out whatever first aid measures could be applied. It was no longer a hospital, merely a motley of fragmented regimental aid posts in the front line of one of the savagest battles in the war. A true disaster was narrowly averted in the remains of the resuscitation ward when a fire started in the straw. Someone with presence of mind took an armful of the blazing stuff and threw it out of the window, preventing thereby a major conflagration.

Then, amidst the uproar, the heavy deep-throated rumble of the approaching tanks themselves could be discerned, the vibration of their tracks transmitted along the ground also being felt through the floor of the building. When it really seemed that nothing could be added in the way of shocks to what had already transpired, one of these monsters, which must have been hugging the pavement, suddenly fired its gun right outside the once glass-fronted ward which had previously served as the hotel dining-room. It was futile to look for any protection from the assault on the nerves that this produced. Every time it fired everyone visibly flinched and jumped. My state of mind was bordering on the hysterical, grinning and bearing it, but with the grin almost exploding into a kind of mad laughter at the sight of all these shell-shocked marionettes jerking and twitching as the tank pulled the strings. The tank maintained its position outside for about fifteen minutes and then clanked on westwards.

No sooner had we begun to enjoy the relative sense of relief occasioned by its disappearance and the cessation of its firing, when the Germans once again burst into the building, this time in far greater numbers, and proceeded with great rapidity and thoroughness to take up positions at all the downstairs windows, in several places poking machine guns offensively through gaps torn in the pitiable barricades the Medical Corps had erected. They were soon all over the place, shouting and threatening, and by their mere overwhelming presence consolidating the subduement effected in us by the bombardment. But with their arrival, catastrophic though it seemed, came respite from the battle. The German advance flowed through, around and beyond the Schoonoord and before long it ceased to be in the front line. The worst belonged to the past. The new situation, although unutterably depressing, stimulated a new response. We were prisoners but still alive and our casualties, considering everything, had been unexpectedly few.

It was now clear the reason for yesterday's lull in the enemy attack had been merely a tactical pause for regrouping and reinforcing their infantry, in order to make a maximum effort in conjunction with a new supply of tanks. Those who now occupied the hospital were from an SS Regiment of the toughest fibre. Aggressive and determined, and preoccupied entirely with the exigencies of battle, they appeared hardly to notice the sorry plight of the wounded, pushing them roughly out of the way to make room for their machine-gun emplacements, and brooking no interference from those Medical Corps men who had the temerity to remonstrate with them.

As though stunned by the avalanche that had overwhelmed us, we doctors at first could make but the feeblest efforts to contend with the appalling situation facing us. The hospital was a crumbling ruin and yet, confined within its battered, shell-torn walls, were some four hundred wounded men in the direst need of food and fresh dressings, as well as the specialized medical and surgical attention their condition demanded. We who had the care of them not only lacked the means, but in some cases the physical strength to administer these necessities, nor could we now move a step without having a weapon of some kind brandished at us. Our captors, in apparent complete disregard of the conventions, were rapidly turning the Schoonoord into a fortified strongpoint, taking advantage of the immunity from British return fire that the Red Cross markings conferred.

With the recession of the battle to the westward, however, there came a gradual relaxation in the attitude of the Germans and we, as we started to recover from the numbing effects of the day's events, were enabled to make a start on the mammoth job of clearing up. The presence of the Dutch ladies, still – incredibly – with us, was invaluable as they bridged the gap of language and acted as interpreters.

Simmons and I, along with one or two others, had been placed under guard in what remained of the theatre, and tried to indicate with signs that our place lay with the wounded upstairs. By dint of repeating the word 'krank' and pointing first at ourselves and then at the ceiling, we managed at last to convey our meaning to the guard who, with a dubious and warning look on his face, opened the door, beckoned with his finger and said, 'Komm.' We went upstairs with the guard following close behind and faced up to the shambles in our ward. Fortunately it had not received any direct shell hits but it was in a terrible state, floor and patients deep in dust and dirt, chippings from walls and ceiling where fragments had struck, and a ghastly mess by the window where a sanitary bucket had been overturned.

'See if you can get hold of some orderlies,' Simmons said to me; 'we'll need an army to clear this up.'

The German guard had departed, perhaps he had not liked the sight and smell, and I descended to the hall to put our request to the control point. There I found an exchange of courtesies taking place between the CO and two German officers, one a Captain, the other a doctor with the rank of Lieutenant, who had arrived in a battered car shortly before. I told control point of the need for more help upstairs, and then my curiosity got the better of me and I hovered on the fringe to hear what Marrable was saying.

Tentatively at first, he requested the German officers to honour their responsibility to the wounded. Now that we had become their prisoners they had the duty of feeding us and arranging for proper treatment. This was quite clear under the Geneva Convention and Marrable soon began to press the point home with gathering asperity. I gained the impression from the way the discussion was going that the Germans themselves were by no means sure they had obtained complete mastery of the battlefield, and were inclined to be accommodating in case there should be a reversal of positions, but when pressed they began to make excuses on grounds of lack of supplies and transport. Marrable played the card of the many German wounded in the building who would testify to the good treatment they had received, and gradually the atmosphere thawed and he felt able to approach the most delicate point of all.

'Under the Convention,' he began firmly, 'it is not correct for a hospital to be used as a refuge for armed troops. It is not correct for your machine-gunners to use this building knowing our troops will not return fire. I demand they be withdrawn.'

Everything seemed to go back to square one. The German officer bridled. 'You are in no position to make demands of me. If you find yourselves in this position you have only yourselves to blame. We do not consider the normal conventions of war apply to you parachute gangsters.'

'But,' said Marrable, keeping his voice calm and even, 'all in this hospital have ceased to be combatants. We have no weapons, and these wounded who wear the uniform of the British army were soldiers, not gangsters. Now they are incapable of fighting and look to you for civilized treatment.' Again he played the card. 'We have treated your men correctly. We ask you to do the same for ours.'

The discussion continued in the same vein for some time and, at one point, we were informed that Hitler had given an order to the effect that paratroops were to be treated as spies and shown no quarter. Hitler, however, was not fighting at the front and, while his troops on this particular front fought as ferociously as any, they showed a respect for their opponents that kept the fight, on the whole, remarkably clean.

Step by step the relationship between prisoners and captors became established on a reasonably civilized and humanitarian footing. The fundamental antipathy between both sides could not be disguised. The points of view, from which each regarded the other, were such poles apart that no common ground could be found, except the impersonal and abstract one of interpreting the correct medical usages of war. Since both parties subscribed, unlike the Russians, to the Geneva Convention, an appeal to its code could be made without fundamental antagonism, and it was here that the areas of agreement were defined. The Germans agreed to remove their armed troops, apart from those guards necessary to prevent the possible escape of lesser wounded back to their units and the fight. They agreed to provide food and medical supplies, and to arrange the evacuation of the seriously wounded as soon as possible. With the reinforcement of the medical Lieutenant by two other German medical officers the atmosphere began to lose its explosive quality, and real strides could be made with the work.

I spoke to one of the German officers in reply to a question about the number of wounded upstairs. Having discovered I understood no German, he tried me in French. We both had enough of that language for simple exchanges and I was surprised and, after what we had been through, rather gratified to learn that this officer, who had seen service in nearly every theatre of war, including Russia, considered this present battle exceeded in ferocity anything he had yet experienced.

'Our own wounded have been very numerous,' he said; 'we have the most extraordinary difficulties. Do not misjudge us if we do not do all that is needed at once.' He pointed to a bandage, 'We have nothing like this. We are now forced to use paper instead of linen, and as for cotton wool,' he turned the palms of his hands outwards and shrugged his shoulders, a gallic gesture induced perhaps by our use of the language, 'it does not exist.'

'No cotton wool?' I echoed. 'What do you use instead?'

'Sphagnum.'

Sphagnum is a kind of dried moss. I had heard of it but never seen it in use. I began to wonder what else they were short of and what sort of treatment our wounded would be getting.

'Have you penicillin?' I asked.

'Only what we have captured from the Allies. We rely on prontosil. Here,' he took out a case and offered me a cigarette, 'here, have a Player. They were for you. We have done well out of the mistakes of your air navigators.'

I accepted the offer, and taking out my lighter snapped it open and proffered it to the German doctor, who cupped his hands round the flame in a friendly way. I lit my own and, lifting my head to take the first deep inhalation, caught sight of my Dutch nurse staring at me from the other side of the hall. She had a look of intense disgust on her face and, refusing to meet my eye, abruptly turned away with a hard set to her shoulders.

'Excuse me,' I said to the German, 'I believe the nurse wants me.'

I hurried after her, puzzled at her demeanour. True, it was some time since we had last exchanged a glance or word. Could it be she thought I had in some way neglected her? I placed myself in her path.

'I say, stop a minute. Why did you look at me like that, is anything the matter?'

'How could you?'

'How could I what?'

'How could you talk like that and accept a cigarette from a German?'

'I don't quite understand.'

Her face was a blend of frustration, anger and disappointment.

'That German,' she hissed, 'he is an enemy. You should not lower yourself to be friendly. They are vile. What do you suppose they will do to us now you are beaten?'

'But we are not beaten yet.'

'They will stop at nothing,' she went on, ignoring my protest. 'You do not know what they are really like. They will take Dutchmen and shoot them as a reprisal. They will take people away to concentration camps.' She gave a little shudder. 'What will become of us now I do not dare to think.'

'He was a doctor,' I said in a voice that implied we doctors were a race apart. 'Medicine has no barriers.'

'He was a German and no better than the rest. You just do not know them and the suffering they have caused.' Her lip trembled. 'The suffering they are responsible for, but will never admit. Our people have endured them for four years; their humiliations, their insults and their cruelties. Only the most detestable collaborator would do as you have just done.'

I was taken aback by the intensity of her feeling.

'But,' I protested, 'we have to talk to them to make arrangements for our wounded.'

'Yes,' she snapped, 'but you do not have to smile at them and accept their cigarettes.'

Her passion was genuine, and I was at a loss to know what to say. But, feeling I could not leave it there, I began to explain hesitantly, 'In England German airmen, shot down while bombing civilians, were given cups of tea by those same civilians if they happened to parachute into their back gardens, and there seemed to us nothing unusual in that. A man should get his deserts, but justice is an impartial thing, it should be the officers of the law who punish him, not the individual; not even the individual he has wronged. This German has not even wronged me. As far as I know he has not wronged anyone. I cannot feel any hatred for him personally for what other countrymen of his may have done. I can't feel it, and I cannot pretend to something I do not feel.'

'You do not feel it because you have not suffered,' she remarked quietly.

'I know that,' I knew she had put her finger on the difference, 'but, as I said before to you, it is so difficult for us in England to imagine what it must be like to be occupied. I assure you we mean to beat the Germans – it is now only a matter of time – and to bring the guilty to justice.'

'Well,' she said, nodding her head to emphasize her words, 'I am very afraid. When you have won the war I hope you will let the guilty Germans be tried by the courts of the countries where they committed their crimes. Let Seyss Inquart be tried and punished in Holland. I am afraid for your British justice. The Germans will congratulate themselves on getting off lightly and in ten years' time, if not before, they will be saying their only crime was to lose the war and be ready to go on the march again.' She tugged my arm. 'Do you not see? We are a small country and they have done terrible things to us we can never forgive or forget. The Germans will always be a menace to our freedom, and we shall not feel safe unless their power is utterly crushed and unless through suffering, as we have suffered, they understand what it is they have done.'

Her eyes began to fill with tears and I moved to put an arm round her, but before I could do so she flung a pointing finger at one of the burly figures in grey green, jackboots planted widely apart, coal-scuttle helmet pulled down over a hard-looking, expressionless face, sub-machine gun held at the ready, and said bitterly, 'Does he look as if he understood what Germany has done? Do you think you will ever make him understand?'

I hunched my shoulders. It was no use. The gulf was fixed. But at that instant I saw something of what she saw as having come out of Hitler's Germany, and I felt a sudden coldness clutching at my heart; I might shortly be going there.

There was a continual tramping of feet along the passage to the service side-door, which the Germans had elected to use because they could park their vehicles on the concrete apron in front of the garage, where the hospital building gave them cover from view from the west. Airborne troops were known still to be in possession of several houses in the hospital area, this much having been ascertained by collecting parties, permitted by the enemy to go out to pick up wounded when the battle appeared to have been stabilized. Whether because they did not know of their presence, or because they were in no hurry to subdue them, the Germans made no attempt to take any action against these houses; neither did the Airborne men take any action at this time against the Germans, although they must have had them clearly in their sights on many occasions.

In the matter of supplies the Germans proved as good as their word, bringing up a van of food early in the afternoon. They also distributed cigarettes, and began to ease the congestion by removing their own wounded and evacuating some of ours. The Arnhem–Utrecht road as far as the hospital, and a little beyond, was safely in their possession and, with their usual thoroughness, they rapidly cleared away the debris to make way for their vehicles which, nevertheless, were obliged to steer tortuous courses around the bomb and shell holes. There was so much to occupy all the workers in the hospital that time passed rapidly, and when Simmons, to whom I felt obliged to apologize for leaving so long in the lurch, and I had brought some order out of the chaos in our ward we found considerable progress had been made in many directions.

Most importantly, negotiations had been going on between our own Senior Divisional Medical Officer and the Senior German Medical Officer in the area, for the purpose of declaring the hospital a neutral area for the rest of the operation. It was a liability to both sides. By its unfortunate position on the crossroad it had gravely compromised the defence of this vital area for, if it could have been made into a strongpoint and occupied by fighting men instead of wounded, the Germans would have found their way barred by a very formidable obstacle. Now the crossroad had been lost, the hospital prevented the launching of an unqualified counter-attack to regain it. From the German point of view, on whom the care of the wounded had now devolved, the same applied. They had agreed and had partially implemented the agreement to remove their fighting troops, and now needed a respite to effect evacuation of the patients. They did not know for certain whether or not the Second Army might get across the river in sufficient strength to push them out, especially during the coming night, and it was preferable for them to use their vehicles for evacuation rather than for constant resupply, as would be the case if the wounded remained where they were. It was, therefore, to the mutual advantage of both sides to declare a neutral zone. The crux of the situation was whether either side trusted the other sufficiently for any truce of this kind to be made to stick.

The negotiations, carried on with the Dutch ladies as go-between interpreters, were very delicate. The framework of agreement emerging was that every house within a circle, one hundred yards in radius, drawn arbitrarily on the map with the Schoonoord as centre would be evacuated by all Allied and German troops, and only those engaged in actual transport or care of wounded would be allowed in the area. Any man requiring treatment would be allowed to enter the zone provided he was unarmed, but having entered would have to accept prisoner status. Eventually it was settled that at 5 p.m. all German troops would leave the area in an easterly direction, and the Allied troops in a westerly, and under no circumstances were either to open fire on the other.

As zero hour approached the atmosphere became very tense. My Dutch nurse, who had been involved in the negotiations, said she was sure it was a German trap to make us give away our positions. I think we all felt the same, but our negotiators must have assessed the risk. There was really no other way. It was the wounded who were calling the tune by their need for better treatment than we could now provide.

The Germans had made a thorough search of the building for arms and satisfied themselves there were none on the premises, except for those already declared to them stacked in the garage. They were to leave their Lieutenant Medical Officer and a dozen German medical orderlies with us until the morning, when it was hoped they would be able to begin the work of evacuation in earnest. The remainder of the armed German sections were forming up in the hall, a formidable looking bunch, while the CO and the rest of us looked on anxiously at the proceedings. The hall echoed with gutteral words of command and the minutes ticked by. At the appointed hour they started to file down the passage to the side-door. Hitherto, those entering and leaving by this door had been unarmed and wearing Red Cross armbands. Now that it was fully armed men about to expose themselves, the sense of apprehension, as each one stepped out onto the garage forecourt, communicated itself to our tense, watching group, and we waited with bated breath until at last they were all out and the door closed behind them. With a sigh of relief Marrable refilled his pipe.

'Phew, I'm certainly glad to see the back of that lot,' he muttered. 'I've no desire to live through another hour like the last.'

The words were hardly out of his mouth when there was a sudden fusillade of fire outside, that froze us all into the attitudes we happened to be in, so we resembled a group of dusty statuary. Again came a fusillade, and another, and another, while none of us moved and none of us spoke, not even when a pounding of feet, followed by shouts and a violent opening of the service door continued the predestined pattern of disaster set by the first shots. One of the Dutch ladies ran up the passage to the door and tried, ineffectively, to bar the way against a scowling, shouting German Sergeant who pushed her before him as though she did not exist. Seeing Marrable, he flung the lady aside, so that she stumbled against the wall, and levelling his gun shouted in a plethora of rage at which the German Medical Officer, who had been standing by immobile like the rest of us, moved swiftly towards the Sergeant and, placing his hand on the levelled gun, uttered the one word 'nein'. Marrable was standing erect, his hands by his side – in one the pipe, blue smoke curling leisurely up from the bowl – never taking his eyes off the Sergeant.

'For God's sake tell me what's the matter with him.'

The sound of his voice was the signal for renewed shouts on the part of the Sergeant, louder cries of 'nein' from the Lieutenant while the Dutch lady, responding to her cue, said in a shrill voice, 'He says he has been fired on by the British. That the British did not keep their bargain. That they are dirty swine, and he holds you responsible and ought to shoot you.'

'Tell him there must be some mistake,' said Marrable calmly.

Meanwhile into the background had crowded the rest of the Germans who had left with the Sergeant, and the two groups now faced each other, ourselves, submissive and apprehensive, and the Germans, visibly enraged, with itchy fingers on their triggers. Between both were placed the Lieutenant and the Dutch ladies, speaking at the tops of their voices in an effort to defuse the situation.

'They say,' said the ladies' spokeswoman, the owner of the hotel, 'you have broken your word. That you are responsible for the shooting and have tried to trick the Wehrmacht.'

Marrable composed his face into a look of sheer astonishment and shrugged his shoulders.

'Tell them it's no use their being cross with me. I have no control whatever over the troops outside this building. They can't have received the order.' Then, spacing his words out, he added with great emphasis, 'They certainly would not shoot if they had received an order not to.'

The lady translated this into German, pointing up the words with downward sweeps of her hand. The German Sergeant thumped his fist on the side of his gun.

'How did they know we were leaving if they had not received the order?' he shouted.

Marrable thought for a moment. 'The answer is simple. They observed you leaving and, not knowing about the agreement, took you for a legitimate target.'

The German did not answer. Seizing the initiative, Marrable continued in an incisive tone of voice, 'Where did the firing come from? Let me see. Show me.'

As he said this he walked straight towards the German group, who stiffened momentarily and then let him pass. The Sergeant, taken aback, lowered his gun and fell into step beside the CO, the Germans closed in behind them and the ladies followed. Without thinking, because the Dutch nurse was at the back of the group, I detached myself and with a few swift paces crossed the hall after her. When he reached the service door Marrable called for interpreters, and so it was that, pushing a way past the Germans for the ladies, I found myself with them, Marrable, the German Sergeant and Lieutenant, by the door, while a solid phalanx of enemy soldiers filled the passage between us and the hall. Marrable, wearing a Red Cross armband, stepped outside while the Sergeant indicated, from the threshold, from which direction the firing had come.

'No sign of anything now,' Marrable murmured to me as he stepped back inside. 'Damn fools. Why couldn't they hold their fire.'

There was a guttural jabbering behind us and the nurse said, 'They are very angry. They say some shots came from somewhere in that direction as well.' She pointed to our right behind the garage. Their main complaint had been of firing from the other side of the Arnhem road. 'They say, unless you can guarantee they will not be fired on again if they leave, they will call up their tanks.'

'Did you hear that, sir?' I said to the CO.

'Yes, I heard. How the hell can we guarantee anything?'

'If they are fired on again they are very likely to do as they say,' she said in a strained voice.

'On the face of it they've every right to,' said Marrable half to himself. 'I should be hopping mad if I was in their place. But can't they see how damn difficult it is to get orders round to every isolated unit after a shambles like this morning.'

She turned and spoke wearily to the German Sergeant, and then said to us, equally wearily, 'He repeats you are responsible. He says they are fighting a war. If you British swine, that is what he says, do not keep to your agreement they will have to take steps to see you are no longer in a position to break it. They will put in a full scale tank attack, and no doubt the hospital will suffer in the process. He says that if it ceases to be a neutral area you have only yourselves to blame.'

'Might they not be bluffing?' I put in in a hopeful voice. 'If the bridgehead is still holding, they must have lost quite a few tanks.'

'They wouldn't need very many to wrinkle out this district,' replied Marrable. 'After all, it's in their hands apart from a few houses. No, my concern is for the neutral area. It is so very much in the interest of the wounded. We must save the arrangements if we can.'

'I tell you again,' said the nurse, shaking her head and frowning at me in disapproval, 'they are very angry. You should not under-estimate them.'

As if he had been following what we had been saying the German Sergeant came out with another sharp outburst. She translated, 'He says he must have your answer immediately. He says his patience is exhausted.'

'Haven't I heard that somewhere before?' said Marrable to no one in particular. 'Nevertheless,' he continued briskly, now addressing himself straight to me, 'we shall no doubt have to do something and do something quickly.'

'Yes, sir?' I said interrogatively.

'As I see it the only thing is to make personal contact with these troops and put them in the picture. I will try and locate the main trouble spot across the road myself. Do you feel like trying to find the other one at the back there?' he jerked his thumb over his shoulder in the direction of the river. 'You have been through that way before.'

I hesitated, again experiencing a curious feeling of precognition, as if the projection of a moving picture had momentarily stopped at a frame, the details of which were already imprinted on my mind.

'I'll have a go, sir, of course.'

'Grab some Red Cross armbands, then, and get going. Good luck.'

'Same to you, sir.'

While Marrable delayed only as long as was necessary to explain to the Germans what he hoped to do, and obtain their consent to our leaving the building, I pushed my way back into the hall with the nurse at my heels and started to don my parachute smock, Red Cross armbands and steel helmet, which I recovered from the officers' cache in the cloakroom. She watched me in silence until I was ready and then said unexpectedly, 'Wait here a moment.'

I began to protest, but putting her hand on my arm she squeezed it urgently and said again, 'Wait here a moment. There is something I want to get you.'

She disappeared up the stairs and soon reappeared carrying a broom. Without saying a word she thrust it into my hand and went out through the front door, returning a few seconds later with one of the large Red Cross flags that had been used to mark the entrance.

'Here,' she said, 'tie this on the broom and carry it with you. It will be much safer.'

'Thanks,' I said, 'but don't you think it's a little unnecessary?'

'No, no,' she said, pressing the broom more firmly into my hand, 'you will not be fired on by mistake if you are carrying this big flag, but it is possible they may not see the armbands.'

I saw her point and we tied the corners of the flag onto the broom handle, and went through into reception together, followed by the eyes of the men on stretchers. Then, because neither of us seemed to have any more to say, I stepped out swiftly into the road with one brief backward glance of farewell. I skirted round the burnt-out remains of our vehicles, which were rusting where they had been parked on the day of their destruction, and began a hesitant and uncertain march down the same road along which I had passed the first evening and returned in that last reckless jeep ride the next afternoon.

The sky was overcast and the air felt heavy and moist. The trees formed a tattered, leaf-flaking roof over my head. The smashed and broken gardens were empty and desolate. With every nerve in my body I sensed I was being observed, and felt one false move might ring down the curtain. The atmosphere of mistrust, so palpable in the hospital, went with me, thickening with every step and increasing my sense of insecurity. I had to fight down a temptation to turn back, and as I picked my way over the broken ground, the road as such being almost unrecognizable, with the Red Cross flag sloped over my shoulder, I wished I was anywhere but on this brittle mission. I had to work my way eastwards and took the first left turn I came to. I did not know exactly where the house in question lay, nor how I would know it if and when I came to it. I looked each one up and down, looking for signs of occupation by our men. As the minutes went by and nothing befell me, I was beginning to feel more confident and to sweat less freely when, without warning, a figure sprang up from behind the garden hedge of one of the villas and, levelling a Sten gun at my chest, said hoarsely, 'Stay where you are.'

I stood, eyes staring out of my head, hands frozen on the broomstick, fossilized by shock, while the other scrutinized me aggressively with bloodshot red-rimmed eyes, his dirty, unshaven face hard with suspicion.

'OK. Who are you and what do you want?' The question came rasping through dry, cracked lips.

'Captain Mawson, RAMC, from the Dressing Station. I wish to speak to your senior officer.'

The other was looking anxiously around, this way and that. 'OK, sir, come on in quick.'

He led the way through the door of the villa into a dark hall where the challenge was taken up by another, who detached himself from the shadows.

'Ruddy Medical Officer, mate,' said the first, 'wants to see Major Wilson.'

'It's very urgent,' I said, sufficiently recovered to make some show of authority.

I was led to the top of the stairs. The inside of the villa was in worse shape than the inside of the hospital, since no effort had been made to clean it up. The floor was ankle deep in debris, a door was broken off its hinges, and in the room beyond I glimpsed the kneeling figure of a single soldier watching through the lattice of a barricaded window.

'Not many of you here?' I questioned.

'Not many – now.'

'My God, I'm a fool to ask that question,' I thought.

The other pointed to a dark opening. 'Down there, sir.'

I propped the broom up at the top of the stairs and cautiously descended, my boots clattering on the wooden treads. It led down to a large cellar, where at one end a group of three or four dirty, unshaven men pored over a map spread out on an upturned wooden box, and lit by a single guttering candle. I looked for insignia of rank and, seeing a crown on the shoulder of one of them, cleared my throat and broke into their hum of conversation.

'Excuse me, sir.'

The Major did not look up and I tried a little louder. 'Excuse me, sir.'

At this the Major turned round to face me, his eyes looking unnaturally bright and luminous against his moustached and stubble-dark face.

'Who the devil are you?'

I repeated my credentials, and then launched into an account of the circumstances that were the cause of my mission. There was a field telephone at the Major's elbow and, as I spoke, my eyes kept wandering towards it, while at the back of my mind the assumption grew that the Major must have known about the neutralization of the area, and so it proved to be. When I had finished he came back at me in a rasping and aggressive voice, his words liberally punctuated with colourful expletives.

'I'm damn well not budging an inch from here,' he stormed. 'The boot's on the other bloody foot. The damned Germans fired on us and that's why we fired back. I told the General it was a fool idea. "After you Claud; no, after you Cecil!"' he mimicked a well-known music hall act. 'What do you doctors think this is, drawing-room tea at the vicarage?'

'Sir,' I ventured, admiration for the Major's fighting spirit quickly tempered by a sobering appreciation of the difficulty of the task I had been given, 'sir, I was given to understand the evacuation of the zone was ordered at the highest level, at the suggestion of the enemy, to facilitate removal of the wounded. They are in dire need of proper hospital treatment.' 'Sir,' I added earnestly.

'You bet the enemy suggested it,' rejoined the Major. 'Nothing could suit them better than to have us out of here without having to fight for it. Well, I'm damn well not moving. It's worth a day's fighting to them.' He glowered. 'We've denied 'em this area for three days. A lot of good men have given their lives for it. Do you think I'm goin' to walk out and hand it to them on a plate because some damn doctors ask me to?'

I began to feel desperate. 'Sir,' I said, my own voice rising, 'we have to do the best we can for our wounded. The facts are we have about six hundred altogether in the area, and I feel I must remind you they are likely to suffer great hardship if the enemy carries out his threat to blow you out of here with tanks.'

At this the Major exploded. 'Blow me out of here with bloody tanks.' He turned to the paratrooper next to him, who smiled broadly. 'Have you ever heard of such a thing? What do you damn well suppose they were trying to do all the morning? We made it so hot for them they had to bypass us. We're a thorn in their side and they damn well know it.' He paused and glowered even more fiercely at me. 'I've still got two Piats working and you can go back and tell the Germans they can bring as many tanks in as they damn well like and I'll blow the whole bloody lot of them out of the road.'

I felt myself up against a brick wall. What could I say? I watched him as he lowered his face to the guttering candle and poked the end of a cigarette into the flame. It would be different if I were Marrable, the rank would tell. The thought encouraged me.

'Sir,' I began again stubbornly.

'Well?' the Major barked, exhaling cigarette smoke furiously.

'Colonel Marrable instructed me to say this evacuation of the neutral area has definitely been ordered by Div HQ and has already been accomplished, apart from your unit and perhaps one other. My CO really commissioned me to pass it on as an order, in case you had not received it, and unless it has been countermanded I suppose it still stands.'

'By heavens,' roared the Major, 'the circumstances have changed and that order is out of date. I will not evacuate while I'm under risk of fire.'

'The Germans have said they will not fire unless you do – '

He interrupted me. 'That's enough,' he was bristling with anger. 'I don't give a damn what the Germans say, and I don't trust 'em more than I would a rattlesnake. I told you. The circumstances have changed.'

He gave me a stony stare which I returned bleakly, my heart in my boots.

'Well, sir,' I said at length, 'could you possibly inform Div HQ, so that I can take their latest instructions back to my CO? As prisoners, this may be the last chance of free communication we shall get with our own side.'

Perhaps it was the sad fact that I was in honour-bound a prisoner, although in reality at this moment free, that stirred the feelings of the Major. Unexpectedly the hard lines round his mouth melted into a grim smile and, taking up the telephone receiver in one hand and waving his cigarette airily at me with the other, he said, 'You are in a hole, aren't you?'

He then proceeded to growl down the instrument while, having transferred the cigarette to the corner of his mouth, he vigorously wound the handle on the side of the set, which jumped about uncertainly on the stone floor. I sat down on the bottom of the cellar stairs and waited anxiously while the Major carried on a noisy conversation, occasionally holding the receiver away from his ear and banging it about with a look of frustrated exasperation on his face. At last he put the receiver down and, muttering at first to himself and then at me, said, 'Damn things. It's time they invented something that worked properly. Tell your CO we will evacuate tonight, provided it can be done without loss. If the Germans so much as fire a pistol, they've had it.'

'Thank you, sir. Thank you very much.'

Needless to say, my relief was enormous. I saluted him and was about to turn on my heel, but paused in the act and asked, in a voice I hoped sounded casual, 'Can you say what you think the chances are of liberation? The Dressing Station's been in and out of the bag once before and we're all hoping this time it's not for good.'

The Major looked at me inscrutably. 'Not a damn chance, I would say. Not a damn chance for you or any of us.'

Then waving an abrupt dismissal he turned again to study his maps. I climbed out of the cellar, carrying in my mind an unforgettable last impression of his indomitable figure hunched like a conspirator in a medieval dungeon surrounded by his henchmen, their shadows dancing on the vaulted ceiling, while the candle flickered in the draught blowing coldly down the stairs.

When I found myself once again by the burnt-out jeeps outside the Schoonoord I found it difficult to credit the villa and the Major had really existed. The whole thing had been like some strange dream from which I was only now awakening. My life had for so long been confined within the physical limits of the hotel building I felt genuinely relieved at being once again in its familiar precincts. It was like a home-coming to normality; but a fantastic normality, epitomized by a tired-looking girl in a crumpled dress standing at the entrance of a battered ruin, while at her side lounged a German soldier, himself in a way imprisoned by the needs of the wounded.

'How was it?' she asked, taking the broom with the Red Cross flag.

'All right. Where's the CO?'

'At the control point. He got back a short time ago.'

I reported to Marrable and he revealed that very much the same state of affairs existed in the other house, occupied by elements of the Polish Brigade. They were prepared to move out if they could do so without loss. Everything depended on neither side firing on the other. There was no way of guaranteeing it since neither side trusted the other, but the German Sergeant was given the assurance there would be no firing if they left the building. Then, since there was nothing more to be done about it, we busied ourselves with the care of the wounded, apprehensively waiting to see how things would turn out.

It was not long before the last of the daylight faded and darkness came to the rescue, spreading a welcome veil over the sights of expectant guns. Half an hour later the Germans filed silently out of the service door while the hospital listened with bated breath for the sound of firing. There was none. Another hour passed without incident. The German Medical Officer and orderlies who had remained behind visibly relaxed. That crisis was over, and in the short time that remained before fatigue called a halt, the Royal Army Medical Corps and the Dutch civilians were able to give their undivided attention to those for whom they had come to be where they were.

Sunday 24 September

Sunday, the beginning of the second week of the battle of Arnhem, dawned all too soon. Utterly exhausted by the tensions, dangers and fatigues of all that had gone before, I had fallen almost immediately into a deep sleep, oblivious to the discomforts of the hard floor on which I had stretched out without even the customary gesture of removing my boots. 'At least,' I had mused as I dozed off, 'we may be spared any further bombardments now we are a neutral area.' Here I had superstitiously touched the wooden floor. 'Perhaps I have come through. The war can't last for ever.' It had seemed to me in my weariness anything, even being a prisoner, would be better than having to brace frayed nerves to withstand any further shocks of noise, of screaming, crashing mortar bombs and tank shells. Above all, having come so far intact, I wanted to stay that way, and stay alive. As if in rebuke the image of the Major in the cellar came into my mind. No defeatism there. Always I seemed to find myself falling short. 'Ah well, I'm only a ruddy Medical Officer. Perhaps they would never have been able to make a real soldier of me.' The next thing I knew, I was being none too gently prodded with the butt end of a rifle and a German guard, who from my horizontal perspective looked gigantic and menacing, saying, 'Aufstehen. Aufstehen.'

I knew no German, but the implication was obvious and I got to my feet with alacrity, surprised to find the owner of the rifle was quite short, several inches smaller than myself in fact, and that his expression was faintly amused and almost benign.

The hospital was rapidly stirring to life, and already the familiar routine of the early morning attention to the needs of nature was in unlovely progress. The smell of the place had, in some subtle way, been augmented by the presence of the enemy so that, in addition to the sickly miasma emanating from urine buckets, pus-soaked dressings and sweat-soiled clothes, there was an unfamiliar blend of foreign tobacco and scented soap, or so it seemed. Possibly the soap was not scented but the enemy just smelt relatively clean and fresh compared with ourselves. I asked Simmons, whom I encountered in the kitchen where officers were forgathering for their customary shave and tea, if he had noticed the difference.

'Can't say I have,' he replied disinterestedly. 'But then I try not to get too near them anyway.'

I proceeded to soap my face in silence. I had brought a Rolls razor with me with a built-in stropping device for sharpening it. The clack-clack it made was a part of those morning ablutions and not too popular with the others; clacker Mawson someone had called me. But I did not mind. There was not one of us without his peculiarities.

'What do you suppose the drill will be today?' I said as I stroked at the stubble.

Simmons was busy cleaning and drying his razor with that intent look that came over his face whenever he was preoccupied.

'Get the serious cases away on the Jerry ambulances and then dilly-dally.'

'Dilly-dally?'

'That's right. CO's working on the idea that, if we can find ways and means of obstructing the evacuation at the point when we're down to cases who won't suffer from the delay, it might be possible to get ourselves retaken again when the chaps counter-attack.'

'Counter-attack? How do the chaps counter-attack against tanks with the little they have left?' I felt there was some kind of game on and I had been left out of the side.

Simmons methodically put his razor in its case and fixed me with a somewhat patronizing gaze.

'They are reinforcing across the river tonight!'

'How the hell do you know that?' I was beginning to feel cross at being so in the dark.

Simmons lit a cigarette and released the smoke in a slow trickle through his nostrils. 'Where have you been? ADMS* slipped in at about two this morning and gave us the gen.'

'Go on for God's sake. What is the gen?'

'The gen is, as I have said old man,' Simmons released another

---

*Assistant Director of Medical Services (Col. Warrack – Senior Divisional Medical Officer).

trickle of smoke, 'there's to be a major reinforcement across the river tonight. A battalion of infantry has reached the south bank and they're only waiting for another mob, and the REs who are bringing up boats, before making their effort. If they succeed in getting across the river they'll counter-attack tomorrow morning. If they don't feel strong enough they'll postpone it twenty-four hours and build up again tomorrow night. So you see it behoves us to hang on here as long as we possibly can.'

I did see and, somehow, I felt immensely irked to find, having resigned myself to being a prisoner of war, hope was again stirring, and there was still to be another fierce battle that might redetermine possession of my person. My immediate reaction to Simmons' news was far from enthusiastic. The let-down already experienced had been too dispiriting to allow me a real belief in a successful outcome now, at all events as far as myself was concerned. Others might be liberated or get away, but not me. I was in the mental condition of one who had accepted his sentence and felt that further appeals could only postpone it without altering the verdict. On the other hand Simmons seemed cocky and assured, but then he always did. One never knew what he was really thinking. They all appeared impervious to fear, doubt or dismay, and carried out their duties with an incorrigible and, to me, sometimes infuriating cheerfulness. Well I, too, would appear cheerful. 'Bang on, Clifford,' I enthused, slapping him on the back. 'Operation dilly-dally. Something to make the kids laugh. When do we start?'

'Right now. The first thing is to get the seriously wounded away as soon as possible. If we seem keen enough early in the day to get them moving we may establish some credit with the Germans so that they may be less suspicious if we try to hold things up later. What we have to do is to go to our ward and mark up all the chaps in order of priority for evacuation, put them in the picture, and then try to hold back every case that can do without special treatment for forty-eight hours. The first lot of Jerry ambulances are supposed to be here at eight o'clock.' He looked at his watch. 'That's in a couple of hours' time. I'll go off and get started now. Join me when you've finished your cuppa and shave. OK?'

'OK,'

In spite of my earlier misgivings, as I completed my shave, I felt myself becoming quite enthusiastic at the thought of the game about to begin, and I made haste to complete my ablutions and join Simmons. He had been giving the wounded an account of what was intended, and spirits had noticeably brightened with something, for some at least, to think about, other than depressing speculations about what would become of them in the hands of unknown German doctors. There was a livening of expressions and a stirring of bodies which, as the morning light increased, made a distinct contrast to the scene of huddled apprehension disclosed by previous dawns. For the first time, it seemed for many mornings, ears were not being strained in anticipation of a bombardment. So that when, at seven o'clock in full light, there came a sound like an express train passing overhead followed by a deafening crump a short way away, quickly succeeded by others, we all gaped at each other in unbelief, immobilized like astonished deer; then, with one accord, those erect dived for the floor and those already lying on it pulled arms, blankets, haversacks, anything handy over their heads. The express trains passed overhead in an unending stream, but after the initial surprise had been absorbed men began to relax and, figuratively speaking, emerge from their hiding places and merely listen.

After a time a Sergeant said, 'Those are not mortars, they're too big.'

'And they're all going over,' commented another.

'It's either Jerries shelling the Div, or the boys on the other side shelling the Jerries,' the first Sergeant continued. 'We've nothing as big as that on this side.' He listened intently. 'Could be twenty-five pounders.' Again he listened. 'I bet anybody they are. That's Monty shelling the Jerries. Blimey! What a lovely sound!'

A croaking cheer went up from the men in the ward. Whether or not all were convinced by the pronouncement of the Sergeant who, being a gunner, carried some authority in these matters, all behaved as if they were. Even I felt sufficiently emboldened to go and look out of the window. The rushing of the invisible shells and their explosion sounded very loud, but there was no sign of anything coming down in the vicinity, on our side at least. Simmons came up and stood at my elbow.

'They may be ours,' I said to him, 'but they sound too damn close for my liking. Hope they know what they're doing.'

Simmons poked his head out of the window and looked around as I had. 'It's no good worrying, old man. If they get our range by mistake we shan't know much about it. Better get on with the work.'

We examined all the dressings, administered drugs to those who needed them and worked out the order of priority for evacuation.

As with so many things in medicine there was a group who un-
doubtedly needed urgent hospital treatment, those who beyond
doubt could wait, and a rather larger group who were much more
difficult to categorize.

We had almost completed our assessments when the shelling
stopped as suddenly as it had begun, leaving an exaggerated silence
in its wake and, very shortly, the call of birds could be heard taking
their rightful place in the scheme of things on a sunny September
morning. Eventually we took our completed records down to the
control point and shortly afterwards the first of the German ambulances arrived, accompanied by a high-ranking German Medical
Officer and his aides. The ambulances scarcely deserved the name,
being a hotch-potch of battered commercial vehicles distinguished
only by large Red Crosses on their sides and tops. They wound their
way jerkily along the torn-up road, following a serpentine and
unpredictable route to avoid the holes, and fetched up in an untidy
line outside the Schoonoord, having first advanced to the crossroad
where they performed a wide, sweeping turn to bring them back
facing the way they had come. The German Medical Officer advanced to the accompaniment of much clicking of heels and Hitler-
saluting by the German guards, who seemed manifestly relieved to
find their responsibility at an end. During the shelling, I was told,
they had appeared far from happy, clamping their helmets more
firmly on their heads and looking uncertain whether they should
watch their prisoners or the terrain outside for a British attack.

Marrable ambled with studied nonchalance up to the senior
German officer, drew himself up into the ghost of a position of
attention and then stood relaxed, one knee bent, while he proceeded
to fill his pipe. The Dutch lady-owner of the hotel, who had come to
perform the office of chief interpreter to the CO, stood by in
attendance, and a short parley took place; the participants looking
for all the world as if they were performing some scene from a play,
the loudness of the German's voice leaving no doubt as to his
identity, the agitated movements of the lady's hands contrasting
strongly with the quiet immobility of the Englishman. When the
conversation had gone back and forth for a while, Marrable raised
his voice and spoke to the company at large:

'The German officer says that he has taken a lot of trouble to place
this fleet of ambulances at our disposal. He hopes we shall return his
consideration by co-operating to the utmost in carrying out his
orders.' He allowed a few seconds for these words to sink in and

then continued conversationally, 'Those ramshackle boneshakers outside are hardly fit to carry a healthy man let alone a sick and wounded one. But I expect it's all they've genuinely been able to scrape together and we'll have to make the best of it. We'll get those on the priority lists loaded up and away as soon as possible. I want no obstructiveness to start with. Right, that's all, carry on.'

And so slowly, imperceptibly, stretcher by stretcher the community of wounded was dismembered, the first of the four hundred taking with them as they went their own intangible measure of that spirit which corporatively gave the hospital its life. For a hospital only exists in and for its patients. Without them it is nothing, a mere shell of bricks and mortar, doctors and nurses as functionless as bells without ringers or shoes without feet. The hospital was dying, shedding its life blood drop by drop through its door. Men, who had lain so long in the same place that they had grown roots through the floor beneath them, felt them tearing as they were rent from the sides of their companions in suffering, and their farewells and feeble protestations rose suddenly, unexpectedly disconsolate, like a lament. I felt extraordinarily affected, standing in the hall, as the stretchers went past the control point to be checked off the hospital roll. I scrutinized the faces to see if there were any I recognized, ones I had had the care of, or members of my battalion, and when every now and again a dirty hand would be thrust towards me and dry lips move under their stubble, 'Goodbye, sir, good luck, sir, thank you,' it was sometimes more than I could do to say anything in return, for fear my voice would be stifled by the constriction I felt in my throat.

With this dissolution of the cement that bound us all together there came a reversal of emphasis upon the individual, upon the parts that had been for so long merged in a greater whole. From the hospital men were going out singly into the unknown, and as we watched them, if my own thoughts were any common indicator, we began to anticipate our own turn and to think speculatively about our own futures. There was an instinctive regrouping, each looking again for the few others with whom they had initially gone into action – those who had jumped in the same stick or flown in the same glider. It was the hospital which had fathered the relationship between Simmons and myself and, much as I regarded him, I felt a strong pull of the older associations that went much deeper than the more recent ones. If I was to be cast adrift from this present mooring I wanted Dwyer and Adams with me and, the idea was forming, I should like to be back with my battalion, with Richard Lonsdale and his force.

Thus, when two ambulance convoys had made the journey to Arnhem and back and were about to begin their third, this compulsion had grown to the point where I had to seek out Dwyer and Adams. We had been going about our different duties in different parts of the building, absorbed into our own spheres of activity with little to remind us of each other's presence. Yet now quite naturally we picked up the old threads again, and it came as no surprise to me when Dwyer, after a few preliminaries, said, 'Funny you should come along just now, sir. I was thinking we had been long enough with this unit and ought to be getting out. There soon won't be anything for us to do here and I don't aim to stay in the bag if I can help it.'

'Agreed. You know about them reinforcing across the river tonight?'

He nodded.

'Had you any plans in mind?'

It was as if we had picked up a conversation in the barn or garage, what to do next. 'Getting out' was not going to be as easy a thing as all that.

'What I think is, sir, as long as we hold the ferry the lads in the perimeter are not going to let themselves be taken. If they can't hold on, they'll pull out across the river. If we can get back into the perimeter we'll either get in for the victory drive or stand a good chance of getting away.'

'There's good sense in that,' I said. 'Major Lonsdale was holding the church by the river, and still is as far as I know. He has some of the 11th with him and I think we should try to join him. The question is, when? In any case I shall have to obtain permission from the CO before I can leave, and we'll want to take Adams, that is if he wants to come.'

'He wants to come all right, sir, I've already asked him.'

I looked at Dwyer's hopeful expression while I thought round the problem of timing. Any movement made outside would best be at last light.

'It might be more favourable to choose to wait until we can be sure how the build-up's gone.' I was thinking aloud.

Dwyer quickly chipped in. 'No, sir, I reckon tonight's the night, and I would be happy if you would ask the CO, sir, and,' he hesitated, 'you don't mind if I say so, sir, but if the CO doesn't give you permission, I think I'll have to have a go on my own.'

'I'll ask him.' I made my mind up. 'But I'll have to wait for a convenient moment. The Jerries've been buzzing round him like flies. I'll let you know as soon as I have spoken to him.'

'OK, sir,' said Dwyer with finality. 'Good luck.'

As I walked away, bent now on seeing Adams, I felt a tingle of excitement, bordering almost on alarm. Dwyer had opened up the idea of our escape in such a matter-of-fact manner that it was only now really coming home to me that it was an escape we were planning, and the penalty of getting it wrong might be very severe. Presumably the enemy was strongly positioned between the neutral hospital area and the perimeter itself, to reach which we would have to run considerable risk of recapture, if not worse. I ran Adams to ground with one of the stretcher parties and spoke to the Corporal in charge.

'Will you spare me Private Adams for a moment, Corporal? I would like a word with him.' The Corporal looked surprised. 'He's my batman,' I added.

'Certainly, sir.' He looked around him. 'Adams, here, you're wanted.'

Adams thankfully placed his end of a stretcher into the hands of another and followed me into a corner where we could talk undisturbed.

'How are things with you, Adams?'

'OK, thank you, sir.'

'Good! You look a lot thinner.'

Adams smiled ruefully. 'Can't put on much weight with this grub.'

'Well, look,' I came to the point, adopting a more serious tone of voice, 'I've been talking to Sergeant Dwyer and he tells me you would like to chance your luck in getting away from here and out of the bag.'

'Yes, sir, I would that. I want to see my wife not the inside of a prison camp.'

'OK. Now I know that's the way you feel, I can say that Sergeant and I are agreed we should try to get back to Major Lonsdale and what's left of the Battalion, but the attempt depends, as far as I am concerned, on what view the CO takes for one thing and how the land lies for another. Don't talk to anyone else about it. I'll get in touch again later.'

I returned to the control point to see if there was any chance of speaking to Marrable. The hall was thronged, a queue of stretchers moving slowly past the check point and out of the main door. He was obviously much too busy to want to give his mind to my project, and so I went out into the road to watch the ambulances being loaded. There were six vehicles and each carried four stretchers arranged in double tiers. One armed German rode with the stretchers and another sat in front with the driver. Four journeys would clear almost a hundred wounded, and I calculated, at the rate things were going, it would not be long before the majority of the serious ones, at least, would have been evacuated. It was now past noon and the morning, apart from the shelling, had passed off uneventfully. There had been an occasional spatter of firing but no battle of any consequence had developed, or even looked like developing. It was a clear day, the sun was shining and fluffy white clouds drifted lazily across the blue sky. It was good to breathe in the fresh air and I stood watching the proceedings for about half an hour, when I was joined by Simmons, who announced quietly, 'I've been trying to find you to say that operation dilly-dally is now in effect.'

I glanced round to ensure we were not overheard and asked, 'OK, fine. What's the drill?'

'Well, in general, just make everything take twice as long as usual; twice as long to get the Germans' meaning if they tell you something, twice as long to lift a stretcher, twice as long to carry it, twice as long to put it down. Bandages must fall off and any other damn thing you can think of tried on. The CO's in dead earnest about this, because they'll pack the more lightly wounded into these vehicles ten, or a dozen at a time, and he fears, when the hospital is half empty they might start moving some of us.'

'Us. You mean the doctors?'

'Yes. They'll probably need our help.'

I stood a little while longer after Simmons had departed, contemplating the scene and wondering if the situation here outside offered any scope for delaying tactics. Letting down tyres and similar pranks were out of the question because the vehicles were too well guarded, but it might be possible to cause some congestion in the doorway by getting a stretcher jammed across it, provided it could be made to look quite accidental. It felt like a game, but in reality every precious minute gained would add to the total sum that would count in the long run, in our bid to postpone our own removal by the enemy.

Thoughtfully I re-entered the hotel. I had certainly been very lucky so far. Compared with the men who fought outside in the woods and streets, dying over their gunsights, my battle had been easy. But how ignorant and foolish I had been back in England, actually chafing to get into action. How completely I had failed to understand what it might mean. I stepped aside to allow another wounded man to be carried out, managing as I did so to jam one of the bearers up against the wall for a few valuable moments. 'There, but for the grace of God, go I. Best not to think about it. Take it as it comes and hope to get out in one piece.'

In the hall my Dutch nurse was hovering in the background of Marrable's group and the sight of her turned my thoughts outward to the painful situation she must be in. The disappointment of the Dutch was too harsh to permit discussion. To have greeted the British as liberators only to find the liberators could not liberate, and themselves now needed liberating, was a terrible reversal of hope and a trial of faith. The destruction of life and property had been to no purpose, as far as they were concerned. They were in a far worse position than before, now having to face the prospect of German reprisals for their co-operation with us. Condolences and apologies were quite inadequate. I could think of nothing I could say to her. The situation was beyond repair. It was appalling and everyone knew it. The steady departure of our wounded had set the seal on the debacle and, although there was much talk of the counter-attack and much store set by it, the fact of men being driven away and swallowed up in the German lines could not be gainsaid. The whole hospital, while hoping for relief, was expecting captivity.

It was with some diffidence, therefore, that I approached her. Her eyes were ringed with dark lines of fatigue and her once confident and uncomplicated gaze was troubled and anxious. She seemed to be leaning entirely on the older ladies, from whose side she had scarcely moved all the morning, and to be completely played out, and no wonder. She had endured everything we had from the very beginning, and that without the prime physical toughness of the trained paratrooper.

'Hallo,' I said, coming up to her slowly.

'Hallo,' she answered, a flicker of a tired smile showing round her mouth.

'Would you like to come outside and have a breath of fresh air?'

The suggestion seemed to take her aback a little.

'Yes, I think I would,' she said hesitantly. 'Yes, that would be a good idea.'

And she followed as I led her down the passage to the side-door, where I stood aside to let her step on to the garage tarmac. I had hoped to find some privacy there, away from the main centre of evacuation, but a burly German soldier lounged towards us from the road, and with a jerk of his tommy-gun motioned us inside again.

'Tell him you feel faint and the doctor says you must have some air,' I said quickly. 'Here, sit on the step and act up a bit.'

She needed to act up very little, being obviously so tired. After regarding us suspiciously the German took up a position a short distance away and gazed in the other direction. I lit a cigarette and placed myself between him and the nurse, putting a foot on the step she was sitting on and resting an elbow on my knee.

'The air gets very bad inside,' I said.

'Yes it does,' she replied.

I smoked in silence and then said cautiously, 'Have you made any plans?'

'Plans?'

'I mean are you going to hang on here or try to get home?'

Pensively she looked down at her feet.

'I had not really thought about it. I expect I shall stay here as long as I am needed.'

'They will have half emptied the hospital by tonight, more than half, and we are afraid it won't be long before they start moving out the officers.'

I was really trying to convey to her my feeling that our presence in some way guaranteed protection for the women. The behaviour of the Germans continued to be very correct, but who could know what would happen when Marrable or Major Frazer were no longer in the place to bring the prestige of rank to bear on the observances of the Geneva Convention. I felt instinctively she should go home now. If the counter-attack succeeded she would be as well liberated in her own cellar as here. If it failed or did not materialize she would be infinitely better off at home, away from the Germans. After some further inconsequential exchanges of conversation I came out with what was in my mind, anxiously watching her reception of it.

'You think then the Airbornes are lost?' was her first comment.

She looked at me directly and threw the words out as a challenge.

'I think the Schoonoord is lost,' I answered obliquely, 'and that it would be prudent for you to get away as soon as you can.'

The afternoon sun dappled through the trees and glinted in her hair, as again she bowed her head and looked at her feet. Suddenly she looked up and laid a hand on my knee and, with a brief glance at the back of the sentry, said to me urgently, 'Could you not come with me? I and my parents could hide you. We have a big house.'

I drew in my breath.

'Oh no,' I said, 'I couldn't do that.'

'Why not?' she pressed me. 'We could get in touch with the underground and they would get you across the river to the Allied lines. They are doing it every day with your airmen.'

I stood up and looked at the Arnhem road. She sounded very certain but it all seemed too easy and unreal. Besides I was already committed with Dwyer and Adams to the move to try and rejoin Lonsdale and I did not want to tell her about that. I turned to her and said, 'I could not possibly involve you in the risk. It would be so dangerous for you if we were caught. After all,' I repeated the well-worn phrase, 'the war can't last for ever, and there are worse things than seeing it out in a prison camp.'

'Do you really want to go to a prison camp?' she almost snorted.

'No. Of course I don't, but nor do I want to be the cause of you or your parents coming to any harm.'

'We will not,' she began the argument all over again. 'The Germans cannot occupy and control the whole of Arnhem all the time, only the main roads and key buildings. They are very short of men now, we know that. They would have no special reason for suspecting me or my parents –'

I broke in. 'They know you are here. Anyone who has worked with us will be under suspicion, won't they?'

She did not answer.

I pressed on, 'You have done more than enough for us already. We got you into this and it would not be right to drag you in any further. We owe you your safety.'

She shook her head, mocking me gently.

'Will I not be safe with you? Why do you look so on the black side? You Airbornes may have failed this time but there is the great victorious Allied army only a few miles away, and a lot of Holland already free.'

I felt the discussion must not go on like this. I had to tell her about Dwyer and Adams. Her reaction was instantaneous.

'Well, they must come, too.'

I was wishing by now I had never let myself bring her to the side-door and question her about her movements. I was getting into deep water. The more she said the more attractive I felt her proposal becoming, yet I knew I had to refuse; but how to do so without seeming churlish, that was the difficulty.

'You don't know how really grateful I am for what you have offered.' I could see from her face she knew from my tone of voice I was going to turn her down. 'But I don't really belong with the people running this Dressing Station. Dwyer, Adams and myself are from a parachute battalion, members of which we believe are still in action down by the church. Now that this place is folding up we ought to try to rejoin them. We hope to try tonight.'

'And if you fail?'

'If nothing worse happens, we expect we will be recaptured and brought back here.'

'Then I shall stay here until tomorrow and if you come back you will come with me.'

She said this with such finality I knew there was nothing more to be said. I squeezed her hand and helped her to her feet, and we went back into the ruined building.

The passive resistance offered to the evacuation was proving more effective than we had dared to hope. There was no scope for overt acts of sabotage, we were too well guarded for that, but by the simple process of going slow the transport of every stretcher was made to take three or four times as long as it had in the morning. When the time of day arrived, at which the British are normally accustomed to take tea, a sit-down strike was successfully organized, the protesting Germans being blandly told that a tea-break was the invariable custom in the British army, even on active service. Once a not too badly wounded patient 'fell' off his stretcher in a groaning heap on the stairs, and it took the doctor a good half-hour to make an examination, removing dressings, bandages and items of clothing to ensure no serious injury had been sustained; during which time, of course, the movement of stretchers up or down was effectively blocked. As the delays multiplied, the Germans became manifestly more and more exasperated. All the bearers were very 'tired' and needed frequent rests. Sometimes they were prodded back into activity by a jackboot, but apart from doing the bearing themselves, which in some instances they did, there was little the Germans could do except urge us on, and urges did not move patients.

I hovered about the hall, trying not to appear conspicuous, anxiously waiting for a suitable moment to approach the CO, who was checking each man out with a German officer and personally taking leave of them as they were carried to the door. At last, during a pause in the proceedings, I saw my chance.

'May I have permission to speak to you, sir, privately?' The army formula came to my lips, and I looked meaningfully at the German officer.

Marrable threw me a nod. 'Why, yes, of course. What is it? Come back in here.'

We dodged under the counter of the reception desk into the control point, and wedged ourselves in the deep recess under the staircase where the wireless operator had normally sat, and there I unfolded my plan while Marrable drew on his pipe. After I had finished Marrable considered for a while before replying, and then removed the pipe from his mouth, meticulously brushing a minute fall of ash from his lapel.

'I fully understand your wish not to be captured. We all share that. I understand, too, your desire to rejoin Lonsdale, and I think that is proper and of more value than going into the bag with my unit, if we go. But there are one or two things that have to be thought of. First, if you were caught while trying to escape you would be breaking an unwritten agreement we have with the Germans and it could react on those obliged to stay. Second, you are not the only officer to have discussed escape plans with me, and I can't have you all disappearing until I'm certain I have no further need of you. I have been given to understand the Germans are going to use us to continue the treatment of our wounded elsewhere, as they are extremely short of doctors in the field. Third, this battle is by no means over, and if they pull it off tonight we can be out of the bag anyway. Another thing, if they did recapture you, they would almost certainly move you straight back further into their lines. It's a tricky situation and we should not do anything premature. Give me some more time to think about it. I'll let you know what I decide.'

I accepted his reasoning and verdict, but if we were going to make the attempt tonight we should need to get it cleared with him before too long.

'I hope your decision will be favourable, sir.'

'I hope so, too,' Marrable said rather sadly. 'You must know I have all your interests at heart.'

Somehow, for the first time, I properly realized the great burden of responsibility he was carrying and I felt sorry to have added to it at this time. I had the feeling, though, that it was going to be all right.

163

He had always understood and regarded my attachment to his unit as temporary, and I felt I might be in his good books after yesterday. I went in search of Dwyer and Adams to put them in the picture. Having rounded them up, we withdrew into the resuscitation ward, now all but empty, and stood by the partly barricaded aperture of the french window.

'We should act on the assumption that the game is on,' I said, 'and be fully prepared to leave at short notice. Let's check over what we think we shall need.'

Dwyer replied without hesitation, 'I suggest Bert scrounges some grub for a start, and a blanket each, and plenty of fags and matches.'

'OK, Sarge,' Adams showed his surprisingly white teeth.

'A torch would be very useful,' I added.

'A bit more difficult that, sir, but I'll have a go.'

I pondered. 'Then there's the question of which way out. There's always a guard at the main exits.'

'There isn't one here,' Dwyer indicated the french window. 'We could be through here and away in no time.'

'There was a German in here last night,' Adams put in quickly.

'Yes, maybe, but it was full of wounded then,' pointed out Dwyer.

'It seems to be as good a way out as any,' I commented. 'I doubt if there will be one here tonight and if there is we could probably get him out by arranging a diversion.'

'No trouble there,' said Dwyer, 'I can easily get one of the lads to raise a rumpus in the next room, nightmare or something, and get somebody to call him out. We can be in here pretending to be busy. I'll get on a stretcher myself if necessary.'

'Have to play it a bit by ear,' I said. 'Where shall we assemble the kit?'

'Dump it in here under a pile of straw. Three large haversacks with blankets rolled and tied on top. Stuff the rest in our pockets and blouses.'

'OK, I'll leave it to you. I'll get in touch as soon as the CO gives me the all clear.'

I was like a cat on hot bricks. Having made a round of the few patients still remaining in my ward, I slipped unobserved into the cloakroom and surreptitiously sorted through my gear. There was a broken window conveniently overlooking the road, and I was able to catch glimpses of the ambulances and loading processes. I stayed there, out of the way, watching, until the time came when the convoy of empty trucks returned for surely what must be the last time. The sun had set, and the Germans had said they would not be continuing the evacuation after dark. Since earlier on, when Simmons had first suggested the possibility of the officers being evacuated, and especially since the plan had been agreed between Dwyer, Adams and myself, I had felt nervous with each return of the convoy. Now I felt my heart thudding against my chest wall as the Germans clanked back into the building. Was it to be patients or officers this time? I waited tensely, and then the stretchers appeared. Patients, thank God. Feeling it was safe to emerge I stepped out and promptly collided with the French-speaking German Medical Officer, from whom I had accepted the cigarette.

'Pardon me,' I said, bowing myself hurriedly out of the way.

The other inclined his head and smiled civilly, while I cursed myself for being a clumsy fool. In my state of mind I imagined anyone could read my thoughts and I went upstairs to the ward again, with the idea that as long as I looked busy I would invite no suspicion. I made myself talk to the wounded, since I could hardly stand about doing nothing. I kept looking out of the window until at last I heard the ambulances starting up and knew we were safe for the night. It was getting steadily darker as the evening light faded. We should have to be going soon. It should not take more than twenty minutes or so to reach the church if all went well, but we should need a little light, not enough to make us conspicuous, but enough to navigate by. I should have to make a move towards Marrable as he had made no move towards me.

The Germans had left fewer guards than the night before but, because the place was now so emptied of wounded, they still made an impression of strength as they stationed themselves, two in the hall, one at each of the usual exits, and others scattered discretely in the downstairs rooms. I glanced into the resuscitation ward, no German in there. I found Dwyer and told him.

'Right, I'll stow the kits in there now.'

I told him where I had put mine in the cloakroom.

'I'll see you and Adams in here as soon as I've tackled the CO. Wish me luck.'

I wished I did not have to approach Marrable. I had been hoping against hope he would send for me first. But the light factor made it absolutely necessary now, and I was not one to like to hang about once I had made my mind up to a thing, especially a thing like this. I had already seen Marrable was positioned at the control point and was threading my way towards it, aware of the great gaps among the rustling figures on the floor, when my ears caught the sound of an approaching vehicle. It was coming down the Arnhem road and, with a final splutter of its engine, it drew up outside the main entrance. I stopped just short of the control point, and a sentry at the top of the stairs, who had moved in haste to look out of the nearest window, shouted something down to those below who hastened to fling open the front doors, jumping back at once to form an impromptu guard of honour for the one who entered. He carried a torch which he now switched on and beamed towards the control point until it picked out the CO. Wanting to know what all the commotion was about, I advanced nearer.

Marrable, who never had dealings with any German except through an interpreter, waited impassively until the lady arrived on the scene. The one with the torch turned out to be the Medical Lieutenant I had bumped into earlier. He conversed with the guards in a relaxed manner until the assemblage was complete and then addressed himself to the CO. The lady translated while I fidgeted, anxious about the time being wasted and with an irrational but growing feeling of apprehension.

'He says he regrets disturbing you.'

'Not at all.'

'You will be pleased to hear the wounded comrades are being well looked after.'

'Thank you.'

'He is personally in charge of many of them.' As he delivered each sentence the Lieutenant leaned back with his hands on his hips to mark the effect of his words.

'Where are you holding them?'

'In a hospital, naturally.'

'In Arnhem?'

'Close by, Herr Colonel. They will soon go to a fine hospital in Germany,' he smiled deprecatingly. 'We have many wounded also.'

Marrable did not smile. 'What is the purpose of your visit?'

'I regret the necessity, but it would be to the benefit of your wounded if we had a German-speaking doctor. They try to resist the treatment we are giving them.'

'Resist?'

'Yes, Herr Colonel. They do not understand we are trying to help them. We need one of your doctors who understands German to explain to them.'

166

Marrable shrugged his shoulders. 'I regret, I have no German-speaking doctors here.'

'Can that be true, Herr Colonel? Are your doctors not well educated? Will not some of them have learned German at school?'

I suddenly felt an icy foreboding.

'I regret,' Marrable repeated, 'I have no German-speaking doctors here.'

The German Medical Officer thrust his thumbs in his belt and looked around him. His eyes met mine and the jaws of darkness closed. I knew immediately what was to happen. With another of his all too easy smiles he strolled over to me and clapped me on the shoulder. 'Ah, my friend. You and I can speak in French together, you can come with me and help me. Splendid.'

Marrable tried to console me but there was no getting out of it. I was allowed to take my leave of Dwyer and Adams, the latter doing me a last service of recovering my kit and fitting me out for my journey. I dressed myself in my camouflage smock and webbing, set the red beret on my head, took the haversack with the food and the blanket and then, with a mournful last look at those around me, drew myself up before Marrable and gave him the smartest salute I could muster.

Outside I was seated next to the Lieutenant in the back of a German staff car. As the engine started into life, I looked back at the Schoonoord and thought I saw a slight figure with fair hair standing in the doorway, but it was now quite dark and I could not be sure. I turned my head back and closed my eyes, and then a voice spoke in my ear.

'Ah well, my friend. Now, for you the war is finished, would you like a cigarette?'

All next morning there were sharp outbursts of firing round the perimeter but the ambulances continued to come and go to and from the hotel, and the day wore on without major incidents. In the late afternoon the sky grew overcast and soon after dark, without warning, the hospital was shaken by the onset of a barrage as great as anything that had gone before, and echoed again with the added rattle and smack of small weapons, and the vicious whine of ricochets. To those who remained it seemed like the blessed trumpet of deliverance, each crash a hammer blow to strike off their chains. But a Gulliver among the Lilliputians might have wondered at their joy, for long crocodiles of stumbling men were feeling their way through the dark woods towards the river, where figures crouched on the bank, and small motor boats plied back and forth, trying to avoid the splashes of white hot metal sewn round them by German Spandaus firing from a hill on their right.

And as the tide of men receded and became a trickle, he would have seen the sky cease to shimmer and glow, and the dark clouds of smoke gradually trail away on the wind. And, if he had watched a little longer until all was quiet, it is possible he might have noticed one or two, or more, figures emerge from a battered building on a crossroad, and dart swiftly out of sight among the trees.

Epilogue

1 December 1979. My personal recollection of Arnhem is concluded, and there is nothing more conclusive to those involved than
a battle well and truly lost. But I have not written 'The End' because
it was also a beginning: the start of a new series of experiences.
Imagining myself to be destined for a life behind barbed wire, a
repetition of dull routines of no particular interest, I was taken
entirely by surprise at the variety and intensity of medical work that
soon came my way, nearly all of it outside conventional prison
camps, until my liberation by the American First Army which
reached me in the heart of Saxony a fortunate few days in advance of
the Russians.

Dwyer and Adams did not get away across the river as I had
hoped. I encountered them both, briefly, in the immediate post-
battle phase when the captured personnel of the Royal Army
Medical Corps were operating a large military-type hospital in
converted barracks at Apeldoorn, north of Arnhem. But we were
soon sent on separate ways and I failed to regain touch. As for the
Dutch nurse, perhaps it will be understandable that, when
eventually I returned to England, I had no wish to dwell on the past.
All my energies were directed to the pursuit of a future career in
surgery where the competition for advancement was extremely
fierce, there being so many doctors demobilized at that time with a
similar purpose in view. I was also cherishing thoughts and feelings
for another lady and, apart from the notes I made while a prisoner
from which this book is largely reconstructed, there was nothing to
give me a feeling of linkage. What we had shared seemed as remote
and buried as the battle itself. I do not know who she was or where
she is.

My Battalion commander has now become Lt-General Sir George
Lea, KCB, DSO. I am currently in friendly touch with Lt-Colonel

Richard Lonsdale, DSO, MC, then second-in-command, but have lost contact with Clifford Simmons who became a distinguished obstetrician and gynaecologist. Lt-Colonel Arthur Marrable, whom I came to hold in high regard and respect, died, I am sorry to say, some years ago.

Forty-seven officers and five hundred and forty-five other ranks of the Royal Army Medical Corps took off for Holland. Many were made prisoner in the very early stages of the battle but continued working throughout. At the end, before dispersal to Germany, some twenty-five officers and four hundred other ranks were accountable as being in German hands, together with over two thousand British wounded. I was one of the fortunates, not only because I was a member of that spirited company, but also because I suffered no injuries and, finally and safely, regained the light of day.